Heritage Discovery Walks in the Midlands

by
Peter Groves

Meridian Books

Published 2005 by Meridian Books

ISBN 1-869922-50-6

A catalogue record for this book is available from the British Library.

Meridian Books
40 Hadzor Road, Oldbury, West Midlands B68 9LA

Printed in England by Cromwell Press, Trowbridge, Wiltshire

Contents

3

Preface

Britain has a rich historical heritage and we cannot travel very far without finding evidence of how that heritage has profoundly influenced the development of our land, towns and villages.

The walks in this book cover some fine Midlands countryside, but they also present opportunities to visit castles, battlefields, nature reserves, museums, churches and cathedrals; to admire fine architecture, and to explore some historic towns. And for refreshment there are some excellent pubs, many with interesting histories.

Most of the walks offer a choice of longer and shorter routes, the latter allowing more time to explore a castle, a museum or other feature during, or at the end of, the walk. Some features you may find so interesting that you will want to make a return visit: Ironbridge, for example, is full of museums illustrating our industrial past that even my three walks in this area cannot fully explore. And some of the other towns where my walks start may encourage more exploration – I think especially of Bridgnorth, Ledbury, Ludlow and Tewkesbury; towns that I always find it a joy to visit.

If you have children with you I hope they will be encouraged to develop a greater appreciation of our country's history and heritage.

Good walking!

Peter Groves

The Routes

All the routes, except when on roads, follow paths that, so far as I am aware, are public rights of way or are permissive paths (such permission can be withdrawn but I think this would usually be unlikely). Every effort has been made to ensure that descriptions are correct and the routes have been carefully, and independently, checked. However, no guarantee can be given that they are error free and that there are no misprints or inaccuracies.

I encountered no serious problems of access on any of the routes, a few difficulties that I reported to the relevant local authority being efficiently dealt with. However, if you do encounter any serious obstructions on rights of way please report them to the Rights of Way section of the local authority (addresses on page 8).

A pair of secateurs is always useful since in our climate brambles, etc. can easily become a nuisance on an otherwise good path. And always have a compass and some basic first aid.

Public Transport

I am not a motorist and all these walks have been designed using public transport. Living some four miles outside Birmingham I have found train and bus services to be perfectly adequate, although the Broadway walk had to be done in two halves. I have given information about public transport services, though if you are starting much further away from Birmingham there may be other services that I have not listed. Some useful phone numbers and websites are given on page 7.

As a precaution I always have a list of local taxi firms with me – plus a mobile phone – although I have never needed to make emergency use of these.

The Pubs

I can recommend all the pubs that I have picked out, especially if you are keen on real ale. There are, of course, other pubs on some of the routes, especially in towns, and some of these may be equally good but are simply ones that I have not visited. However, I don't think you will be disappointed in my choices. Sadly, pubs do sometimes go out of business, or change hands, so I cannot guarantee that some of my information may not go out of date. The Good Beer Guide, published by the Campaign for Real Ale, is an excellent source of information and I have marked with **(GBG)** pubs that were shown in the latest edition when this book went to press. However, I feel that several of my pubs, not in the GBG, really ought to be there.

Another good recommendation comes from the Cask Marque scheme, promoted by a group of brewers but independently monitored. A Cask Marque accreditation is given to the landlord and indicates that cask beers are well looked after and dispensed. I have marked a pub whose landlord is currently qualified with **(CM)**.

Maps

My sketch maps are intended as a guide, not to replace Ordnance Survey maps which you should always have with you – preferably the Explorer series which are much more useful to walkers than Landrangers. Although I hope this will not happen, there is always the possibility that you might need to change your route because of bad weather or some unexpected incident, such as a fallen tree completely blocking a path; a footbridge washed away in a storm, or a collapsed riverbank.

Flood Hazards

The rivers Avon, Severn and Teme are featured in a number of walks and these, together with some minor streams and rivers, are prone to flooding after heavy rain. A call to Floodline (see under 'Useful websites and phone numbers' on page 7) may be helpful but it is sensible if you are walking at such times to have an alternative route in mind and to look out for escape routes in case of a sudden rise in water level. Riverbanks are sometimes subject to subsidence.

Towpaths

Few canal towpaths are rights of way but British Waterways permits, and indeed usually encourages, their use by walkers and cyclists. It does mean, however, that when a towpath is closed for work on the canal there may be no diversion, such as is usually provided by the local authority when a right of way has to be closed. Another good reason why you should always have map and compass with you!

Muddy Boots

I always carry a pair of boot covers (available from many outdoor shops) and put these on when visiting pubs and other buildings featured in these walks where muddy boots would not be appreciated. Also I usually have a pair of light shoes in my rucksack.

Useful websites and phone numbers:

Floodline: This provides information about flooding and threats of flooding. However, the absence of flooding on roads and in residential areas does not mean that footpaths are clear.

www.environment-agency.gov.uk/subjects/flood/floodwarning
0845 988 1188

Rail enquiries:

www.nationalrail.co.uk
08457 484950

All forms of public transport

www.traveline.org.uk
0870 6082608

All forms of travel, both public transport and road

www.transportdirect.info
At the time of writing this site was still in development. It is very ambitious.

Business information (I use it for taxi phone numbers)

www.scoot.co.uk

Maps

www.streetmap.co.uk

Canal information

www.britishwaterways.co.uk

Tourist Information Centres

Bridgnorth	01746 763257	Malvern	01684 892289
Broadway	01386 852937	Stratford-on-Avon	0870 1607930
Hereford	01432 268430	Tewkesbury	01684 295027
Ironbridge	01952 432166	Warwick	01927 492212
Ledbury	01531 643313	Worcester	01905 726311
Ludlow	01584 875053		

Acknowledgments

I am very appreciative of all the help that I have received in preparing this book from numerous sources. I have had valuable information from local authorities, museum staff, Tourist Office staff, clergymen, shopkeepers, publicans, and other walkers. I have consulted local guidebooks and church and cathedral guides; and have also gathered information from various excellent websites.

My especial thanks must go to two people who have carefully checked my walks: most has been done by David Milton, but I am also appreciative of my son Nigel's help.

The photograph of the bowman on the back cover is by courtesy of Warwick Castle and is gratefully acknowledged.

Local Authorities and Rights of Way

Gloucestershire
Shire Hall, Westgate Street, Gloucester GL1 2TG.
Herefordshire
Public Rights of Way Manager, Highways and Transportation,
P.O Box 236, Hereford, HR4 0WZ
e-mail: rightsofway@herefordshire.gov.uk.
Leicestershire
Environment and Heritage Services
Community Services Department
County Hall, Leicester Road, Glenfield, Leicester LE3 8RJ.
e-mail: footpaths@leics.gov.uk
Staffordshire
Staffordshire County Council, Martin Street, Stafford, ST16 2LH
Shropshire
Shropshire County Council, Shirehall, Abbey Foregate, Shrewsbury SY2 6ND.
Warwickshire
Warwickshire County Council, Countryside Recreation, Montague Road,
Warwick CV34 5LW.
Worcestershire
County Hall, Spetchley Road, Worcester, WR5 2NP.
e-mail: countryside@worcestershire.gov.uk.

1

Vital Waterways

Stourport

Special Features: The Historic Town of Stourport and the once important link between the Staffs & Worcs Canal and the River Severn; Hartlebury Castle and County Museum: (A walk only),

---

Distance: A: 9.25 km/5¾ miles; B: 7 km/4¼ miles.
Start: Stourport, The Staffs. and Worcs. Canal, York Street (GR812715).
Maps: Explorer 218; Landranger 138.
Car Parking: Riverside Park, Martins Way, off New Street(GR807713); Hartlebury Common, Lower Pooland Car Park(GR826714). If starting from here begin reading from ✪ on page 13.
Public Transport: Rail and bus services to Kidderminster, then bus service from Kidderminster bus station to Stourport. Leave the bus in York Street, walk back down the street to the canal and cross the road to reach the start of the walk.
Terrain: One hilly section but nothing very strenuous. Canal, river, fieldpaths and an attractive converted railway line.
Refreshments: The White Hart in Hartlebury, and numerous other pubs in Stourport and along the canal.
❗ The section through Hartlebury Common proved quite difficult to describe because of the multitude of paths. It has been carefully checked but the instructions do rely on a number of waymarks. If one were to disappear that could create a difficulty. It would be especially sensible therefore to have a map and compass with you and to avoid doing the walk when visibility is poor.

The Pubs

The Bird in Hand
A fine canalside inn, opened in 1772, that still retains much of its traditional character. Four cask ales, including one guest ale.
The Angel Inn (CM)
A welcoming and traditional riverside pub (Banks's) with food, three cask ales and two cask ciders.
Ye Old Crown Inn, 8 Bridge Street. **(GBG) (CM)**
In spite of its name this is a typical modernised Wetherspoon's pub. Lacking character but with the usual Wetherspoon's excellent range of cask ales.

The town of Stourport was created in 1766 when the construction of the Staffordshire and Worcestershire Canal was authorised by Act of Parliament. It opened in 1772, being engineered by James

Brindley, and joined the rivers Trent, Mersey and Severn. It proved to be very successful and the bustling town rapidly developed where the canal joined the Severn. It still retains much of its eighteenth century architecture.

From the canal bridge in York Street walk along the towpath for about 600 metres with the canal on your left, passing The Lock Shop and an old canal tollhouse, dated 1853. Very soon pass the Rising Sun (on the opposite side), some old canal company cottages, dated 1800, and reach the Bird in Hand pub. After passing under the next bridge immediately turn right and ascend steps (or go up the recently constructed rampway) to reach the old Leapgate Railway Line marked by a Welcome sign from the Worcestershire Countryside Service. The line ran from Stourport to Hartington and has been converted into a walkway.

At the top turn left and walk along the walkway, now a fine nature reserve with good views from the embankment, later going through a beautifully wooded sandstone cutting. Follow the walkway for about 1.75 km/about a mile, crossing en route a viaduct over the River Stour. Just after going under power lines and approaching a bridge, turn off to the left, ascend and swing right to cross the bridge.

Follow a bridleway forward across vast fields and soon reach Charlton Lane. Turn right along this for a few metres to reach the B4193 and cross this carefully.

As you will see from the map the B4193 will take you directly to Hartlebury Castle. However, I do not recommend joining the road here since just ahead there is a very nasty bend with no pavement. Also my less direct route will take you past the remains of an interesting old mill.

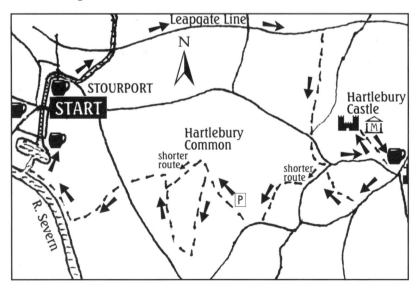

10

Across the road turn left for a few metres, pass the entrance drive to Charlton House and then go right along tarmac passing Charlton Coach House, Charlton Farm House and Charlton House Farm. Approaching a house turn left along an initially paved path into woodland, soon passing a derelict cottage. Cross a stile and walk through a garden swinging round to pass pools and a fine water wheel (this is Charlton Mill), then pass under a footbridge and go through a gate onto a road (Hillditch Lane).

Here the A and B walks separate. For the shorter walk B turn right along Hillditch Lane and now continue reading from ★ on page 12.

Continuing walk A turn left along Hillditch Lane for a few metres, then turn right along the B4193, crossing it *very carefully* to walk along the rather narrow pavement on the opposite side. After about 400 metres meet a drive on the left into Hartlebury Castle, the home of the Bishops of Worcester for a thousand years.

Hartlebury Castle *is on the site of a manor house that was known to exist in the thirteenth century on land given by the King of West Mercia to the Bishop of Worcester in the ninth century. This evolved into the castle, some early parts of which, including the fourteenth century Great Hall, remain today.*

In 1642 the castle was garrisoned for the King and its fortifications strengthened but on 16 May 1646 after only two days and without a shot being fired, the castle surrendered to the Parliamentary army. After some use as a prison for Royalist captives the castle fell into disrepair until in 1675 Bishop Fleetwood began

Bishops Palace, Hartlebury Castle

11

the rebuilding of the castle, work that was continued by his successors.

*In 1964 the north wing of the castle was used for the creation of the **Worcestershire County Museum**, and this was opened to the public in 1966. The former servants' quarters now houses permanent exhibitions illustrating the past lives of the county's inhabitants from Roman times to the present with displays including Roman Worcestershire, Victorian room settings and a Transport gallery.*

(County Museum 01299 250416 open Feb-Nov, Mon-Thurs 10.00-17.00; Fris & Suns 14.00-17.00; Bank Holidays11.00-17.00. Castle State Rooms 01299 250410 Tues, Weds, Thurs during Museum season).

Turn left along this tree-lined avenue to reach the Castle, where there are also opportunities for refreshment. The Museum is housed in the old stable block: note its fine sundial.

Leave the Castle and return to the road, turn left along this passing what is presumably an original gatehouse to the castle. Reaching the White Hart car park (with Hartlebury Church facing you) turn right along Chadwick Lane. After about 350 metres (about 75 metres after passing a hedge gap on the right) cross an easily missed stile on the right and walk slightly right towards the leftmost of a row of small trees (an apple tree). Here swing left

aiming towards a pylon in the middle distance. Arriving at a hedge corner go diagonally right (away from the hedge) aiming now towards another pylon. Reaching trees go down easily missed steps to the road (Hillditch Lane) and turn left along this.

★ *Here the A and B walks re-join.*

After about 250 metres, where the lane bends left, take a path on the right beside a board welcoming you to Hillditch Pool and Coppice. Follow this attractive path through woodland until it brings you out onto Hillditch Lane again. Turn right along the

The path through Hillditch Coppice

12

lane for about 100 metres and, after crossing a stream turn right beside another Welcome sign and, passing the pool on your right, approach a post inscribed 'No Fishing' with a seat a little way beyond it. Just before reaching the post turn left along a path ascending into woodland.

✪ The path emerges onto Hartlebury Common at the Lower Pooland car park where there is another Welcome sign, two horse ride waymarks (the first of many) and an information board.

If you are starting here walk back a few metres and then turn right between the Welcome sign and the horse ride waymarks

Otherwise swing left between the Welcome sign and the waymarks. Soon pass another horse ride sign on your left and after about another 50 metres meet a crossroad of tracks with numerous horse ride signs. Here go forward for about 150 metres to reach another horse ride post.

Here the A and B walks separate again. For the B walk continue reading from ❀ on page 15.

Continuing walk A turn left, aiming towards an electricity pylon that can be seen ahead and is our next objective.

***Hartlebury Common** is popular with horse riders and walkers and there is quite a maze of paths, not reflected by Ordnance Survey maps. I have tried to make the route instructions as foolproof as possible but you may, in places, find it difficult to decide whether you are exactly en route or not. However, once you have reached the pylon the rest of this section on the common consists of two almost straight lines, the first bringing you south-south-west to almost reach the A4025, the second then going north-north-west to reach the corner of a housing estate. Even if you stray somewhat on the first line you are unlikely to approach the road far from the intended point. On the second line it may be easier to miss the target but if you keep an eye open for the housing estate over to the left you should not have a problem.*

The softness of the sandstone on Hartlebury Common means that the numerous bridleways do not become churned up with mud as is a more common experience. However, in places the soft sand will slow your pace, as on a dry sandy beach.

Following the track pass to the right of three posts, two carrying waymarks, the third marked 79, and soon reach the pylon. Pass this on your left and descend into woodland, passing another pylon. Approaching the main road, and about 50 metres before reaching it, swing right onto a grassy area and continue forward.

Look out for green woodpeckers for whom this is a good habitat with plenty of food in the plentiful gorse and heather.

Stay on level ground along a well used bridleway keeping a ridge on your right and soon passing under twin power lines at a point about midway between the pylon on the left and the one on the right (passed earlier). Try to maintain a straight course, avoiding turns off, and soon pass through a traffic barrier of wooden posts.

✳ *The A and B walks rejoin again here.*

From the traffic barrier continue forward for about 25 metres and then turn left on a path which swings right to reach the corner of the housing estate. Turn left here to pass the estate on your right and walk through woodland. Pass a path on your left (leading to housing) and then at a Y-junction of paths take the left fork to reach the A4025. Cross the road very carefully and go forward into a grassy area. Follow the path to Power Station Road and turn left along it. Pass a road on the right and then, when Power Station Road swings left, go right towards a white house and along the tarmac pathway on the right of the driveway beside the house.

The housing on the right was built on the site of an old power station, hence the name of the road.

Reaching the River Severn turn right, now following the Severn Way. Cross the River Stour where it joins the Severn, soon reaching The Angel and a little further on a former hotel The Tontine, now converted to housing. The Tontine was built to provide accommodation for boatmen who worked the waterways when the Severn was a vital route for trade and industry. How much traffic could be taken from our over-stretched road system if the Severn could regain some its former activity!

Stourport Canal Basins

Opposite The Tontine cross a broad lock (taking river boats) by the right-hand set of gates and swing right to cross a bridge and walk beside the river. Cross another bridge and turn right to walk beside a narrow lock (taking canal traffic). The path brings you to a dry dock: here turn right to cross a bridge by another narrow lock, then go left to cross another bridge, then right to go back towards The Tontine, ascending steps or a slope.

*We are here at the **Stourport Canal Basins** where canal and river traffic join, with broad locks for river craft and narrow locks for canal boats. Once a hive of commercial activity it is now busy with pleasure craft and has a lively boat club.*

At the time of writing some very intersting developments were planned for the area of the canal basins so there may be more to see than I have described here.

Cross a broad lock to reach The Tontine, turn left in front of a British Waterways office and turn right to walk around one of the canal basins, noting all the signs of its earlier importance. Just before reaching a road turn left down steps and continue round the canal basin, noting the Clock Warehouse over to the left. Join the road beside an old crane passing on the right some eighteenth century workmen's cottages carrying plaques stating 'This building is an ancient monument and of special historic interest'. Turn left along York Street passing the canal where the walk started.

Reaching cross roads turn right along High Street to reach the bus stop, go forward along New Street to return to the car park, or turn left along Bridge Street to reach the Ye Old Crown Inn on the left or the Bridge Inn on the right.

B walk

❀ Turn right for about 15 metres to meet two paths on the left, one at right angles and the other joining diagonally. Take the first path and go forward through heather and an open grassy area.

You are here aiming due west to meet the edge of a ridge that runs north-south.

Very shortly cross a track and meet another track that runs along the edge of the ridge. Now go forward and descend, immediately being faced with a Y-junction of paths. Take the right-hand one and descend steeply (with a small upward hump). As you descend look out on your right for a housing estate which is our next objective but which soon goes out of sight behind trees. At the bottom of the slope go forward to reach a broad track. Turn right along this to reach a traffic barrier of wooden posts.

Now continue reading from ✳ on page 14.

2

Black Country Regeneration

Wombourne

Special Features: Baggeridge Country Park, Staffordshire Railway Walk, Himley Nature Reserve (Woodland Trust).

Distance: A: 14 km/8¾ miles; B: 12.5 km/7¾ miles.
Start: Baggeridge Country Park Visitor Centre.
Maps: Explorer 219; Landranger 139.
Car Parking: Baggeridge Country Park Visitor Centre (GR900932) (Pay and Display).
Public Transport: Bus WMT256 (Stourbridge/Wolverhampton) or WMT260 (Merry Hill/Wolverhampton). If coming from Stourbridge leave the bus at the stop before Wombourne Church, just after the bus turns into Gravel Hill from Common Road (GR875927). If coming from Wolverhampton leave the bus at Wombourne Post Office. Walk down Gravel Hill (south-east) to cross a bridge over a stream, then turn left along Rookery Road. Now start reading from ❀ on page 21.
Terrain: Some hills, but nothing particularly strenuous; field paths, woodlands, former railway line.
Refreshments: Baggeridge Country Park Visitor Centre; The Round Oak; Wombourne old railway station; The Red Lion.

The Pubs

The Round Oak
A popular Banks's canalside pub with extensive dining facilities. The usual two Banks's cask ales and possibly a guest ale in the summer.
The Red Lion (CM)
Wombourne's oldest pub. It was built in the early 1800s and although now extended still retains much of its original character. Food and some good cask ales.

Baggeridge Country Park is a beautiful area of countryside on the doorstep of the Black Country. The land was originally owned by the Earl of Dudley who lived at nearby Himley Hall. In 1895 coal was discovered at the northern end and pit shafts were sunk. The pitheads were located either side of the campsite near to the present visitor centre. At the height of production it was claimed to be the world's biggest and most modern pit. It closed in 1968.

The derelict land was bought by the council (now South Staffordshire District Council) and designated a Country Park. Government Grant Aid enabled improvement works to be carried out and reclamation began in 1981. The Park was officially opened by HRH Princess Anne on 17th June 1983.

The visitor centre includes a display illustrating the history of the park.

Baggeridge Country Park is open from 9am until dusk every day, except Christmas Day. Tel: 01902 882605 for details.

Passing the Visitor Centre on your right follow the sign 'Start of Trails, Himley Hall and Pools'. On your right is the Baggeridge Country Park Sensory Garden and ahead a picnic area with a metal sculpture and an old colliery wagon.

The aim of the Sensory Garden is to concentrate on movement, sound, feel and smell, emphasising colour, texture, fragrance and light.

For the B walk continue forward with the Events Field on your left and the metal sculpture on your right. Very soon pass a path on your left and continue with woodland on the right. Reaching a crosspaths and wooden rails turn left with the rails on your left along what is described as an easy-access route. This swings left, then right, soon reaching a crossing track and continuing forward. Reaching steps on the left turn down these to reach another track and turn right to descend with a pool on the left, very soon passing a track on the left and now joining the A walk. Continue reading from ✪ on page 18.

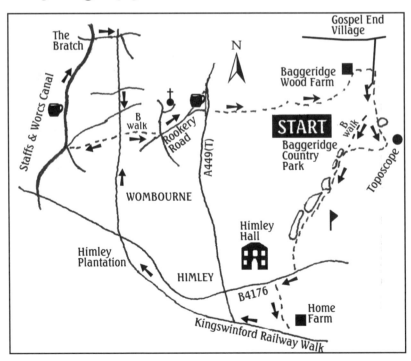

For the A walk swing round on tarmac to the left, passing a toilet block and then, following the signpost direction to 'Himley Hall, Pools and Toposcope', reach a traffic barrier, with a play area and a miniature railway on the left. Then, just before another traffic barrier cross a small grassy area on the right into a parking area. Go straight forward, keeping the parking area on your right, go through a third traffic barrier on the left and descend along a stony path.

Go under a bridge and then swing right, passing Bag Pool on your left (or you may like to walk around it) and reaching a sign 'Toposcope Trail'. Here walk up what was an old colliery tip along a partly stepped steep path and almost at the top go left to reach the toposcope where, if the weather is good, you will have wonderful views of the surrounding area. Now return to the path that you left, turn left along this and descend, partly via steps, then immediately go forward between two grass covered colliery mounds. Descend two steps to reach a track, go right along it to meet another track. Turn left along this and soon turn right at a Y-junction.

You are now on the Baggeridge Circular Walk. Stay on this for just over 50 metres, ignoring paths off, and, reaching a Y-junction, take the right fork. Meeting another track turn right along this and cross an old quarry road. (*When I first walked here it was possible, about 50 metres from the Y-junction, to turn right and go down some steps, then to cross the old quarry road. However on more recent visits the steps had been closed off, presumably because they were dangerous. If they have been repaired then you could use them.*) Go forward along a track which swings left to a T-junction. Turn left here, signed 'Himley Hall and Pools'.

✪ B walk rejoins here.

Soon pass a bridge on the left, cross a bridge and walk with a stream and two major pools (Upper Wishing Pool and Lower Wishing Pool) on your right. After passing the second pool swing right at a cross-tracks and

One of the pools in Baggeridge Park

18

descend to pass a footbridge on the right and soon join another track coming in from the left to walk along the side of Spring Pool. Almost at the end of Spring Pool look out on the left for the remains of the Earl of Dudley's watercress beds. Keeping to the edge of the pool pass a seat at the end of the pool and, just before reaching a 'Health Risk' sign turn left down steps and walk with the stream on your right soon passing a golf course on your left.

Past Island Pool follow the sign to Himley Hall, now on tarmac, passing Rock Pool where if you wish you can briefly take a path beside the pool, returning to the main track after passing two seats. This takes you to a road along which you turn left, then past Ward House with its clock tower on the left turn left, away from Himley Hall and follow the road as it forks left to leave Himley Park at the gate house.

Himley Hall was built in the eighteenth century when a medieval manor house on the site belonging to the Earl of Dudley was demolished to make way for a great Palladian mansion. The 180 acres of grounds were designed by Capability Brown and included a lake fed by a series of waterfalls from the chain of smaller pools that we have just been walking past.

The Hall, a Grade 2* listed building, was popular with members of the royal family: in 1934 the Duke and Duchess of Kent honeymooned here and the Prince of Wales (later Edward VIII) spent his last weekend here before his abdication.

During World War II the Earl of Dudley made the hall available as a Red Cross Hospital. At the end of the war the hall was sold to the National Coal Board from whom it was jointly bought by Dudley and Wolverhampton Council in 1967, being taken over fully by Dudley MBC in 1988.

Turn right along the main road and after 200 metres cross the road carefully and take the track signed Home Farm. Pass the farm and descend to enter, through a white gate, a work yard area. Continue forward to reach a bridge carrying the Staffordshire Railway Walk. Just before this turn right and walk up to join the walk near to a metal plaque. Turn right to follow the railway walk noting the wonderful variety of trees that line your route, after about three-quarters of a mile passing the site of Himley Halt and a picnic area.

The Staffordshire Railway Walk. The Kingswinford Railway was owned by the Great Western Railway Company. Opened in 1925, it served the rural areas to the west of Dudley and Wolverhampton with stations at Wombourne and Himley.

The line was not very successful. Passenger services were withdrawn in 1932, the line being used only for goods traffic, except for a short period after the D-Day landings during World War II when it was used to ferry wounded soldiers to local hospitals. It was closed in 1965 and has been converted into the railway walk by the South Staffordshire Council.

There is a wonderful variety of wild life along the walk with over 280 species of wild plants, many birds, some twenty-two species of butterflies, badgers, foxes, stoats, weasels and other small animals.

Now walking north, first pass through the Himley Plantation, a nature reserve and an ancient, mostly broadleaved, woodland covering about 24 hectares/60 acres owned by the Woodland Trust. Pass under a road bridge to leave the nature reserve and continue through a delightful wooded cutting. Walk for about a kilometre/three-quarters of a mile and after passing under a bridge that is preceded by a short tunnel cross tarmac and continue along the Railway Walk for about 350 metres.

Meeting a crossing path (with a green barrier/gate on the right) the A and B walks separate once more. *For the B walk turn right and now continue reading from ☆ on page 21.*

Continuing the A walk turn left and descend to walk beside the Wom Brook, very shortly crossing a footbridge to walk with the brook on your right. At a Y-junction continue forward, now leaving the brook, to reach and turn left along a road, crossing to the right-hand side. Turn right to cross Giggetty Bridge, descend to the towpath of the Staffs and Worcs Canal (see page 9) and turn left along this to soon reach a road and the Round Oak pub.

Bratch Locks from one of the side ponds

Continue along the towpath, passing Bumblehole Lock, with its unspoilt lock-keepers cottage, to go under Bratch Bridge and reach the three Bratch Locks, a great favourite with visitors.

Bratch Locks are closely spaced with the usual side pounds replaced by two large pools connected to the locks by culverts. These pools act as reservoirs to take and provide water as the locks are emptied and filled. Going through the locks is a rather complex operation and a lock keeper is required. Without his supervision a boat could find itself in a lock completely drained of water!

Return to Bratch Bridge and cross it, then walk along Bratch Lane to pass the impressive Victorian Severn-Trent pumping station.

The Bratch Waterworks were formally opened in 1897, the year of Queen Victoria's Diamond Jubilee. Power was provided by two steam engines that were fuelled by coal unloaded from the canal at the wharf just below Bratch Bridge. They were replaced by electric power in 1960.

Built in red brick, with red, buff and blue brick decoration the building is a fine example of Victorian Gothic. The four corner turrets give it the somewhat incongruous appearance of a Scottish castle. It is sometimes open to the public.

Shortly reach a bridge carrying the Staffordshire Railway Walk. Go under this and turn left to walk up to the former Wombourne station where there is now a pleasant café. Turn left along the walkway, crossing the bridge and walking for about a kilometre/three-quarters of a mile to reach the crossing path on which you left the Railway Walk earlier. Turn left on this.

☆ *B walk again re-joins here.*

Go through the green barrier/gate and bear right to walk with the Wom Brook on your right.

The grass in some of the areas around the Wom is cut only once a year to provide shelter and provision for wildlife (more detail on an information board to be reached shortly).

Soon cross a footbridge and continue along the other side of the Wom to reach a picnic site and a bridge where you leave the brook at a crossroads.

❀ *Bus travellers start here.*

From the crossroads walk north-east along Rookery Road, immediately passing some attractive cottages, one of which is interestingly named Paupers Cottage. Reaching the narrow Battlefield Lane continue forward along this until reaching another junction.

For refreshment at the Red Lion turn left along the road for about 50 metres to reach the pub on the left. Then return to Battlefield Lane.

*We are here on **Battlefield Hill** which could be the site of the Battle of Tettenhall. This was fought successfully by Edward the Elder of Wessex against the invading Vikings in AD910. However, there is considerable uncertainty about its actual location.*

Cross the road and go forward along a short path to reach the dual carriageway of the A449(T). Cross this carefully, go through a kissing gate to join a track and go along this into a field. Walk through the field with a hedge on your left, heading towards a pylon and then passing under power lines.

At the end of this long field pass a post carrying a multitude of waymark signs and cross a stile to enter and walk thorough a wood. Meeting a ruined building turn right and pass the remains of a fine wall. Ignore paths off and emerging from the woodland go straight across a field, crossing a track to enter and pass through another stretch of woodland. Enter an open area where you have a good view of the Clent Hills to the south.

The track swings left to reach Baggeridge Wood Farm. Pass the farm along a path that branches off from the track. Cross a stile, swing right to cross a track and join a path leading into woodland and then into an open area. Go forward, passing a seat on the right to reach an information board describing Gospel End Common, a valuable heathland, now being regenerated, which became part of Baggeridge Country Park in 1970. Past the board the path swings right to meet a track along which you turn left to join a road at a traffic hump. Turn right along a wooded path which runs parallel with and a few metres to the left of the road. Pass through an opening in a wooden fence, turn left, then immediately right and swing left to enter an open area, walking with the road on the right.

Very shortly, at a traffic barrier, swing left away from the road, a tall factory chimney (Baggeridge Bricks) soon appearing briefly on the left, and then swing right to reach the Baggeridge Country Park Visitor Centre where there are refreshments and toilets.

Bus travellers now read from the start on page 17.

Path in Baggeridge Park

3

Civil War Skirmishes

Ledbury

Special Features: The ancient market town of Ledbury with its many historic buildings and museums. The home of the poet Elizabeth Barrett-Browning.

Distance: A: 12 km/7½ miles; B: 9.5km/6 miles.
Start: Ledbury Market Hall (GR711377).
Maps: Explorer 190; Landranger 149.
Car Parking: Bye Street, Ledbury GR710376.
Public Transport: Buses and trains to Ledbury. If arriving by train go down the station approach, turn right to go under the railway bridge and start reading from ★ on p 25.
Terrain: Some steep slopes. Road walking through Ledbury, otherwise one quiet lane and good paths through woodlands, meadows and orchards with some fine views.
Refreshments: Pub in Wellington Heath; numerous pubs and teashops in Ledbury.

The Pubs

The Farmers Arms, Wellington Heath
The Farmers Arms has its origins in a medieval farmhouse which became a cider house: the original cider press can still be seen in the garden. At one time meat was also sold there and hams were hung from the beams in the present lounge area. Chickens were kept in the loft! It was extended about a hundred years ago and the restaurant added more recently. It is obviously popular with diners and has some good cask ales.

The Prince of Wales, Church Street, Ledbury
A lovely timber-framed sixteenth century building, popular with visitors and locals and providing good food and cask ales and also draft Herefordshire cider and perry.

The Olde Talbot Arms, New Street, Ledbury **(GBG).**
This black and white hotel dates back to 1596. There was a skirmish in the fine oak-panelled dining room between the Royalists and the Parliamentarians during the Battle of Ledbury. Food and good cask ales.

Leave the Market House and walk north along The Homend on the right-hand side of the road admiring the variety of architecture and the many timber-framed buildings. Much of this market town would probably still be familiar to those who lived in Tudor times.

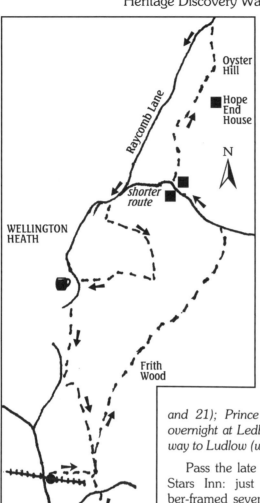

The Homend was the scene of the first skirmishes in the Civil War Battle of Ledbury on 22 April 1645. Prince Rupert, whose Royalist army had reached Leominster on their way to Shrewsbury, learned that the Parliamentary forces, led by Colonel Massey had advanced to Ledbury. He determined to cut them off so marched all night, arriving on the morning of the 22nd. Massey hurriedly assembled a barricade in the Homend but after fierce fighting this was broken and his army soundly beaten. Massey and the remnants of his forces made their way to Tewkesbury (walks 20 and 21); Prince Rupert's soldiers rested overnight at Ledbury and then made their way to Ludlow (walk 16).

Pass the late sixteenth century Severn Stars Inn: just past it are three timber-framed seventeenth century shops. A little further on is the early seventeenth century Abbey House. Next to it is the seventeenth century Horseshoe Inn with opposite the seventeenth century timber-framed Abbey's Bakery. Beside the Horseshoe Inn is Smoke Alley with an old street number plate (43-65). This was originally Smock Alley, probably because some of the inhabitants made smocks. In 1871 it contained fourteen homes, housing sixty-one people and the change of name may have resulted from the smoke from so many chimneys in such an enclosed space. Ledbury has a number of these alleys and resembles Tewkesbury in this respect (see Walk 20) although Ledbury's alleys are now less apparent with many of the original buildings having been demolished.

Just before reaching Tesco opposite pass Cruck House; note the cruck on the gable end – a split arched tree trunk that provides the frame for the building. Meeting Knapp Lane, the large house on the opposite side of The Homend and to the left is Knapp House, the birthplace of John Masefield, Poet Laureate from 1930 to 1967. Reaching the railway, pass the station entrance and go under the bridge.

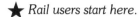 *Rail users start here.*

Turn right to cross a stile and with a fence on the right walk up through an orchard of cider apples followed by a field. Cross a stile on the right and go right along tarmac for about 50 metres and then, just before the track bends right beside a house, turn left to pass a Forestry Commission sign and ascend a permissive path. Ignore all paths leading off and continue through fine woodland to join a broad track. Continue forward along this to walk through Frith Wood, admiring if you are here at the right time of year the many wild flowers, including wild orchids, that line its edges. Soon pass Little Frith Walk joining from the right.

The track eventually starts to descend with good views opening up to the left and reaches a Y-junction of tracks: here take the left-hand option and after passing a path on the left leave the wood to walk between hedges. Pass to the side of a gate reach a road and turn left along this. As the road swings round to meet a large house 'Tattersalls' look over the wooden fence on the left to see, in the valley, the Ledbury railway viaduct, built in 1860. Very soon go through a limestone cutting and pass Hope End Stables with its horse-headed entrance gates.

Here walks A and B separate. For the shorter B walk continue along the road for about 300 metres to reach a Y-junction and here turn left, joining the A walk coming in from the right along Raycomb Lane. Then continue reading from ✪ on page 26.

Continuing the longer A walk turn right onto the entrance drive to Hope End House, cross a stile on the left and follow a path through meadowland, initially keeping a wire fence a few metres on the right. The path swings away from the fence and soon passes the walled garden of the house. As you pass the nearest point to this you have a good view of the Malverns (British Camp) beyond.

Hope End House *was the home of Elizabeth Browning from the age of three when in 1809 her father bought the 475-acre estate in the secluded valley. The picturesque setting inspired some of her poetry: in* The Lost Bower, *published in 1844, she recalled:*

> Green the land is where my daily
> Steps in jocund childhood played;
> Dimpled close with hill and valley,
> Dappled very close with shade;

Summer snow of apple blossom
Running up from glade to glade.

Her father, who later became High Sheriff of Herefordshire, had the house rebuilt in a Turkish style and the gardens landscaped. The estate became a tourist attraction but unfortunately much of it was later destroyed. The present building can only be briefly glimpsed through the trees. Following a decline in their fortunes the family moved away in 1832.

Past the walled garden the path now swings right to follow the edge of Berrington Wood. Cross a stile and walk between a fence and Berrington Wood, soon crossing another stile to reach Oyster Hill with views of the Abberleys and the Malverns ahead. To the west you should, on a clear day, be able to see the Black Mountains. Bear slightly left, passing a seat and a trig point on your right, to descend towards woodland and leave the field in its far left-hand corner.

Cross two stiles and follow a track through woodland – Coddington Church can be seen through the trees – to reach Raycombe Lane. *On the right is a cylindrical concrete structure. A metal cover on the top reads 'B W Rushworth Ltd, Well Borers'. From inside there is the sound of running water so presumably it is a well. I wonder if it supplies water to the rather isolated houses hereabouts.* Turn left along the lane, extensive views opening up to the west with another view of the Black Mountains. Follow the quiet and peaceful lane as it gently descends to Wellington Heath and passing on the left the unspoiled Raycombe House with its fine arched windows. Reaching a Y-junction the shorter B walk joins from the left.

★ About 40 metres past the junction a seat thoughtfully placed in the wall on the left gives a good view of Frith Wood. On reaching Swallow Farm Stables and Rare Breeds Centre turn left and cross a stile beside the gate, followed by another stile, and walk with a fence on the right. Reaching another stile don't cross it but turn left, walking with a hedge on the right and descending. Ahead is another good view of British Camp. Cross two stiles and then go through a patch of woodland. Cross a third stile, pass a gate and turn right through a gate into a field to walk with a hedge on the left and Frith Wood ahead. After a fourth stile cross a track, continue with a hedge on the left, then cross two stiles with a footbridge and go forward across a field, aiming for a gate approximately in the centre of the facing hedge. Go through this and turn right to follow a path between a hedge and a fence. Cross a stile and a footbridge and continue with a stream on the left to cross another stile. Turn right and walk up through a field towards houses, passing to the right of a power pole.

Leave the field by a stile and follow a path between hedges to reach tarmac and turn left along this, passing a small public garden and reaching the entrance drive to the Farmers Arms in Wellington Heath. From the inn follow the road past houses until it swings sharply right, here go a few metres left to cross a stile and walk with a house named Long Acre on the left. Go down to the far left corner of the field – across to the left are two former oast houses, Go through a gate and walk with a fence and the stream that you followed a little earlier on your left, soon crossing a stile. After about 100 metres cross a footbridge on the left, noting the warning to beware of horses, and enter an orchard.

Turn right to follow a track which swings left through the orchard. After about 50 metres it swings right towards a road, then goes left parallel to the road and reaches a gate with the road to the right. Here turn left along a tarmac track and, just before reaching a house, turn right, then right again along a waymarked track to walk through another orchard aiming towards a house in the shelter of Frith Wood ahead. When you meet a wire fence keep to the left of it. On a recent visit the trees carried an excellent crop of cherries and I was able to buy some in Ledbury.

Just to the right of the house go through a waymarked gate and walk through the garden of the house, leaving it by a stile. Now, keeping a fence and woodland on the left go under power lines and through a hedge gap to reach the far boundary of the field and a waymark post.

Turn left over the stile that you crossed earlier and then right along tarmac, passing the outward route. Reaching a road, cross this, ascend steps and continue forward along a wide path through Dog Hill Wood, now following Green Lane, an old packhorse road to Worcester. At a crosspaths continue forward with a seat on the left. Descend steps to join a road, go forward along this and when it bends right go forward to an enclosed path that will take you into the churchyard of Ledbury Parish Church.

Ledbury Church, *dedicated to St Michael and All Angels, is partly Norman. It merits a visit, especially for its collection of monuments and some beautiful windows, one dating from 1991. The floor is paved with memorial slabs from the seventeenth to the nineteenth centuries and these provide a good impression of the lives of Ledbury citizens of those times.*

There is a particularly interesting feature in the nave – if you stand in front of the nave and look up to the roof near the east window you will see what appears to be a red light. This is a small red window that, it is believed, was put in in the sixteenth century at the time of the Reformation. It had became forbidden to have red sanctuary lamps and it appears that someone had the ingenuity to keep up with old tradition in this way.

There is an interesting Norman doorway with chevron mouldings and grotesque faces in the west front. The north porch is Early English and the inner door contains bullet holes that resulted from a skirmish here when Prince Rupert's forces surprised those of Colonel Massey.

The church has a detached bell tower dating from the thirteenth century. It contains a delightful carillon that plays at 9am, 12noon, 3pm and 6pm and which you will doubtless have an opportunity to enjoy if you have timed your walk appropriately.

There is much more to see in the church than I have space to describe here and the church guidebook is well worth buying.

Leave the churchyard by the main gate where, before going forward along Church Lane, you might like to first turn right into the Walled Garden where there is a post made from oak from Dog Hill Wood, erected for the 2002 Golden Jubilee, when fifty English oaks were planted in Ledbury.

Church Lane, Ledbury

Now walk along the cobblestones of Church Lane. This medieval street has many fine buildings and is greatly valued by film and television producers. Of especial note as you walk along it are the Heritage Centre, the Butchers Row Museum, the Prince of Wales pub and the sixteenth century Painted Room in the old council offices. Plenty to keep you occupied at the end of your walk, or perhaps on another visit to Ledbury.

The Heritage Centre *is also known as the old grammar school. It is easily recognised by the jettied first floor, a typical medieval feature and was built in the late fifteenth or early sixteenth century. Look out for the boy's names scratched into the window glass and carved into some timber panels. These date from 1770.*

The Butchers Row Museum *is one of a row of fifteen houses and shops, many of them butchers, that ran down what is now the High Street. They were bought by public subscription in 1830 and one or* two were re-erected. *The museum contains reproduction helmets and breastplates as worn in the Battle of Ledbury in 1645 together with a small collection of musical instruments ranging from a 'hurdy-gurdy' to a Tibetan pipe fashioned from a thigh bone. It is open daily from 11am to 5pm from Good Friday to the end of September and at weekends only in October. Admission is free, but there is a donations box for those who feel it worthy of support.*

The Painted Room. *During refurbishment of the council house a rare painted room of around 1560 was uncovered. It is thought that the room was used to house prisoners in Tudor times. The paintings were of verses from Psalm 15, no doubt designed to encourage them to reform: 'That in his heart regardeth not, malicious, wicked men: but those that love and fear the Lord'.*

Ledbury Market House and the Clock Tower of the Barratt Browning Institute

Returning to the Market House, on the opposite side of the road is the Barratt Browning Institute with Clock Tower.

The Market House was built, probably by public subscription, between 1617 and 1645. It was used, principally as a corn market, by local farmers. The builder is thought to have been the carpenter to Charles I. The ground floor is still used as an open market and the upper floor for public meetings.

The road to the car park is opposite, but for the Olde Talbot Arms, and to see a little more of Ledbury turn left along High Street. A little way along Boots now occupies an old timber-framed building; here cross the road by the pedestrian crossing to St Katherine's Hospital. *This was founded in 1232 as an almshouse, and for tending the sick and providing accommodation for travellers.*

Turn left to pass the Feathers Hotel. *This was originally two sixteenth century cottages; it became an important coaching inn in the nineteenth century and the projecting lantern is a relic of those times.*

Reaching a crossroads the large timber-framed building on the opposite corner is Ledbury Park, late sixteenth century with some later additions. *It was commandeered and used by Prince Rupert as his headquarters during the Battle of Ledbury.* On the right-hand side of High Street is New Street: The Talbot is a little way along on the left, passing on the corner a timber-framed building known as 'The House on Props' because of its jettied first floor. Just beyond The Talbot on the right-hand side is an impressive early seventeenth century timber-framed building with two gables.

References: Ledbury Town Guide; Ledbury Walkabout; Ledbury Alleyways and Yards Trail. My acknowledgements for the help that I have had from these. They are available from the Tourist Office and recommended reading if you would like to spend some more time exploring this interesting town.

4

The Final Battle

Worcester

Special Features: Worcester Cathedral; the 1651 Civil War battlefield; The Commandery Civil War Museum; Diglis Canal Basin; Royal Worcester Porcelain Works.

Distance: A: 12.5 km/7¾ miles; B: 10.75 km/6¾ miles.
Start: West side of Worcester Bridge (GR846547).
Maps: Explorer 204; Landranger 150.
Parking: Worcester. Car park off A44 New Road, by Worcester Bridge. (GR846547).
Public Transport: Rail and bus services to Worcester. From Worcester **Foregate Street station** walk towards the city along Foregate Street, take the second road right (Angel Street), then left along Angel Place to reach Crowngate.
From the **bus station** walk up Angel Row and turn right to reach Crowngate.
From Crowngate walk along Angel Place, then right along Broad Street, continuing into Bridge Street to reach and cross Worcester Bridge.
Terrain: Rivers, canal and field paths. Some tarmac but mostly quiet lanes. One short steep climb on walk A, otherwise flat and easy walking.
! A section of path under the bridge at Powick is prone to flooding and is best avoided when the River Teme is high, even though it may not be over its banks elsewhere (see ◆ on page 33.)
Refreshments: Pub at Powick; plenty of pubs and other refreshment opportunities in Worcester

The Pubs
The Red Lion, Powick (CM) (Walk A only)
A listed building which at the time of the Civil War was used by the Parliamentary forces as a hospital. Its detailed history is not known but it has probably been a pub for 300 years or more. A welcoming pub with good food and several good cask ales.
The Salmon's Leap, Worcester
This lacks the historical interest of the Red Lion but it has good food and five cask ales, including some local brews.

The Battle of Worcester. Following the execution of his father in 1649, Charles II landed in Scotland on 23 June 1650 and in the following summer invaded England. However, his army was under-equipped and underfed and was not having the support that Charles expected. He decided therefore to halt at Worcester hoping for the support of the Welsh Royalists. The small Parliamentary garrison withdrew after token resistance and Worcester's fortifications were repaired and extended.

On 27 August Cromwell arrived at Evesham with a force of 30,000 men and the following day crossed the river at Upton-upon-Severn. A second force was positioned to high ground east and south of Worcester, from Elbury Mount to the Ketch Inn (page 36). On 2 September bridges of boats were constructed over the Severn and the Teme, near to their confluence (page 33). The following morning an outpost of Charles's Scottish troops was attacked at Powick (page 34) and driven back to the Teme. Charles, who was watching from the Cathedral tower rode down to Powick to encourage the defence but two divisions of Cromwell's troops, using the bridges of boats, attacked from the rear; the Scottish defence rapidly collapsed and the men were forced back to the city.

Charles attempted a counter-attack but this failed and the Scots were forced to retreat, the retreat soon becoming a rout. A terrific slaughter occurred at Sidbury Gate (page 36) as the Scots tried to escape into Worcester. Charles managed to slip through and rode down Friar Street to his lodgings and fled with a small group of followers.

After fleeing north, and hiding in the famous oak tree at Boscobel House, he made his way south and, after hiring a

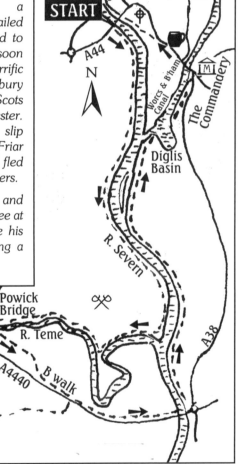

boat, made his way to safety in France: in 1660 he returned to reclaim his throne.

From the western side of Worcester Bridge, and facing the Cathedral, (*observing the large numbers of swans that are usually to be seen here*) go through a gate (not down the steps) and along Bromwich Parade to walk with the River Severn on your left. As a plaque by the steps explains, the Severn was the main commercial artery of the West Midlands, linking to the sea at Bristol. Follow the path for about 3 km/1¾ miles, passing on the right extensive playing fields and noting some of the features on the opposite bank that will be encountered on the return journey, including a slender spire, all that remains of St Andrew's church, known locally as the Glover's Needle; Worcester Cathedral; Diglis Hotel; and the junction with the Birmingham and Worcester Canal. A barrier in the river is designed to prevent boats meeting disaster over Diglis Weir; just past this is Diglis Lock on the far side of the lock island. To the right there are views of the Malverns.

The open land on the right here is Chapter Meadows: as an information board explains this is an area of land that, due to its regular flooding by the river, has been unchanged since records began, so allowing wild life to thrive. It provided a source of hay and then, after this had been cut, was grazed by cattle.

When you reach the end of the surfaced path cross a stile and walk through three fields.

◆ *If the rivers are running high but you still want to carry on you could avoid the risky section by turning right along Weir Lane to reach the A449, turning left along this, then where it bears left take the minor road (Old Road) on the right to Powick Bridge. However, you would probably not be able to do the B walk because that could have a similar problem a little further on.*

On reaching a City of Worcester triangular seat around a stone pillar leave the Severn and turn right, signed to Powick Bridge, to walk along the River Teme, more views of the Malverns soon appearing ahead. Follow this meandering river until you reach a fence with a gap in its centre (originally there was a gate here) with stiles a few metres to either side of the gap and a water trough close to the left-hand stile. Here, go over towards the right-hand stile, make a U-turn and continue beside the Teme; this has made a massive meander and now appears to be heading back towards Worcester with a good view of Worcester Cathedral and the Glover's Needle. The area around here was, as described on a plaque soon to be encountered, the scene of some of the fighting in the English Civil War.

The river swings away to the left – continue to follow it, aiming towards a tall chimney to reach Powick Bridge built in 1837 and carrying a fine coat of arms, the origin and significance of which seems to be unknown. One of the items on the coat of arms is a trow which would suggest that Severn trows would sail up the Teme to Powick. Go under the bridge and carry on

Powick Bridge

forward towards the tall chimney and cross a stile to reach the old Powick Bridge, passing a memorial to the 'thousands of Scots, both Highland and Lowland who fought … in the Battle of Worcester 3/9/1651' It was unveiled by Tam Dalyell M.P. in 2001.

The chimney was part of the first major hydroelectric installation in the world, Worcester City Corporation having converted an old mill in 1894. It comprised four water driven turbines and three steam engines. After becoming inadequate for the needs of the City it was replaced and became a laundry. This closed in the 1970s and the building has been converted into residences. It is worth making a brief detour to view both the front of the building and an old railed vehicle that originally ran on an overhead gantry and was used for lifting heavy equipment.

We are now back to the River Teme and are in the the area (as described by a plaque on the left, just past the bridge) where the first skirmish of the Civil War in 1642 and the last major battle in 1651 were fought. The sandstone bridge was built in the fifteenth century with its first two arches crossing the Laugherne Brook and then three arches at a skew crossing the Teme. Cross the bridge (do not go off to the right half-way across the bridge).

Here walk B separates. For walk A now continue reading from ✪ *on page 35.*

Following walk B, after crossing the bridge take the stile on the left and follow the path that shortly takes you under the A449 again. Walk beside the river until it swings away left, then continue straight forward to reach a fence corner. From here go diagonally right towards the road embankment and turn left to cross a stile beside a gate. Walk forward beside the embankment to pass a bridge carrying the A4440 and reach a stile on the left where you join up with the longer walk. Now continue from ✳ below.

✪ Continuing walk A go down the tarmac drive ahead and on approaching the road swing right to go through a gate and walk, initially by the side of the Teme, waymarked Public Bridleway, but then aiming left across rough ground towards a bridge under the A4440. Here go through a gap in the barbed wire fence and forward under the bridge.

Cross a stile and go slightly right towards the tree-lined fence ahead, then walk with this fence (and a ditch) on your left as it swings left, then right and reaches a stile beside a metal gate.

Cross the stile and walk up the steep slope ahead (Ham Hill) with a fence on the right, then ascend steps and swing away from the fence to cross a stile by a gate. Walk forward along a ridge and very soon pass a stile on the right. Continue along the ridge admiring the fine view over to the left and soon descending steps. Now follow the undulating path until a stile brings you out by the side of a booster pumping station.

Walk forward keeping the booster station on your right to reach a stile and Powick village, passing a spring on the right. Pass Kings End Road on the right and *carefully* cross one lane of the A449 to reach a grassy island, then go along the other lane of the A449, *carefully* crossing to the left-hand side. When the A449 swings right continue forward to reach the Red Lion.

Continue along the road for about 25 metres and then turn left to the twelfth/thirteenth century St Peter Powyke Church. In front of the church entrance turn left and go through the churchyard to leave it by a kissing-gate. Immediately turn right down steps, being greeted if you are walking in the spring by the scent of wild garlic which grows abundantly here. Cross a footbridge and a stile to enter a field. Go forward a few metres, then turn right to cross the field, passing under power lines (rather nearer to the right-hand pylon than to the left-hand one) and reach a metal gate in the boundary fence ahead. Do not go through the gate but turn right beside the fence to leave the field through a gate. *If you look back you will see Powick Church and will have another view of the Malverns.*

Continue through the next field and leave this by a stile beside a gate on the left, go forward under a bridge carrying the busy A4440 and turn right to reach a stile on the left.

Here walk B rejoins.

✳ Cross the stile and turn right to walk with the A4440 on your right. At the far end of the field cross a ladder stile, turn right to go up to the main road, noting the flood level on the left, and turn left. Cross the bridge over the river where, if the weather is clear, you should on approaching the end of the bridge be able to see the Abberley Hills to the left with, between the two main hills, the Abberley Clock Tower. Greeted by a City of Worcester sign immediately turn left to reach a stile on the left; cross this and drop down under the bridge to reach the river and turn right along it, passing under the bridge once more. *On your right is The Ketch Inn where, nearby, some of Cromwell's forces were positioned before the Battle of Worcester.* Walk along the edge of a caravan park, leaving it at the left-hand edge of a row of conifers. We are now on the Severn Way.

Descend steps to walk beside the river, soon passing a sign 'Caution, river bank liable to subsidence'. *I have had no problems, but you should walk carefully.* The path now passes through delightful woodland. Reaching some old gateposts the path splits and here turn right away from the river. Shortly reach a footbridge over the Duck Brook on the left, cross this and soon rejoin the Severn to continue your journey back to Worcester. *If you are walking in the blackberry season you should soon find a good crop. Himalayan balsam seems to be taking over much of the riverside here.*

After about a kilometre/half a mile reach Diglis Lock, the former importance of which is immediately apparent from its size and surroundings, with two-way working for river traffic. Now walk along tarmac and when the road swings right, cross a footbridge over a boat dock. Reaching another lock and a sign showing river and canal distances to Birmingham, Stourport, Tewkesbury and Gloucester, turn away from the river and walk beside Diglis Bottom Lock, signed Birmingham 30 miles, 58 locks. Past Diglis Top Lock turn right beside the Diglis Basin.

Diglis Basin. Here the Worcester & Birmingham Canal joins the Severn and you will see signs of the former commercial activity with broad locks for river craft and narrow locks for canal narrowboats. Today it is largely used by pleasure boats, some of them sea-going. The canal was completed in 1815 and allowed coal and industrial goods to be brought down to Worcester, some then to continue along the Severn to Bristol. In return, grain, timber and agricultural produce went to the developing towns of the Midlands contributing to the growing prosperity of the region.

Cross a swing bridge and turn left around the basin, cross another swing bridge and just before reaching the road turn left passing river craft, canal boats and the garden of The Anchor pub, then swing right to walk along the towpath of the Worcester & Birmingham Canal.

After going under bridge 3 reach Sidbury Lock, swing right to make a U-turn away from the lock and reach the road. On the left is the Commandery with the option here of a break to immerse yourself in the history of the Civil War as it affected Worcester. On the bridge over the canal is a plaque recording information about the last battle of the Civil War, fought in Worcester in 1651.

The Commandery. During the final battle of the Civil War the Commandery housed the headquarters of the Royalist Army. It is a medieval building and until the Reformation was a monastic hospital, established in 1085 by St Wulstan. It then became a country house with alterations being made in the seventeenth and eighteenth centuries. At the end of the nineteenth century it was a college for blind boys and then a printing works, until being purchased by Worcester City Council. It was restored and enhanced and opened to the public in 1977: it now houses a magnificent museum devoted to the Civil War.

From the Commandery cross the road *very carefully* (it is not at all pedestrian friendly and the nearby traffic lights do not have a pedestrian phase), turn right and then left along the No Through Road, passing a motorcycle shop on your right. At a T-junction turn left passing the Royal Worcester Porcelain Works, where the Visitor Centre is open to the public.

The Commandery

Royal Worcester Porcelain. *In 1751 a group of local businessmen established a porcelain manufactory on the banks of the River Severn. From the beginning, great emphasis was placed on superb craftsmanship and by 1789 the quality of the work was held in such high esteem that George III granted the company the prestigious 'Royal Warrant' as Manufacturers to their Majesties, thereby allowing the word 'Royal' to be added to the name.*

From the Visitor Centre there are guided tours of the working factory and you can visit the Museum of Worcester Porcelain and the Manufactory (where you can paint your own plate). There are three Factory Shops where porcelain and many other quality items are on sale. Open daily Mon-Sat: 9.00am-5:30pm; Sun: 11.00am-5:00pm. Closed Christmas Day, Boxing Day, Easter Sunday. Phone 01905 21247 for more details and admission charges

Opposite is the Salmon's Leap pub. Pass King's School, then the Diglis Hotel to regain the riverside walk, turning right along it (Kleve Walk, named after the German town that is twinned with Worcester).

At this point if you wish to return to the car park, missing out the Cathedral, continue along Kleve Walk back to Worcester Bridge.

At the end of a row of horse chestnuts turn right through an impressive gateway (Watergate), noting the flood level records on the right. Ascend some steps and turn right up the road (*passing a gate on the left into the Cathedral Precinct Gardens, that you may like to visit*) and then turn left beside the Cathedral. Go forward under the early thirteenth century Edgar Tower, the gateway to Cathedral Green built by the order of King John and still possessing the original massive wooden gates. Turn left up steps to reach the front of the Cathedral.

Worcester Cathedral. *There is evidence that there had been a Christian community at Worcester since at least the seventh century, but the first cathedral on this site was part of a Benedictine monastery established in AD983. Partially destroyed in 1041, rebuilding was started by Bishop Wulfstan towards the end of the eleventh century. A crypt has survived from this period and is the largest Norman example in England. The restoration was largely completed by 1218. Building continued until the monastery was dissolved in 1540 after which the cathedral suffered extensive destruction and damage.*

Worcester Cathedral

Attempts at repair were made during the eighteenth century but it was not until 1854 that restoration transformed Worcester Cathedral into the magnificent sight that it is today.

Inside are some fine Victorian sculptures, beautiful medieval carvings, superb stained glass windows, and the elaborately decorated tombs of King John, who signed the Magna Carta and who died in 1216, and of Prince Arthur, elder son of Henry VII. At times the sumptuous Chapter House dating from the early part of the twelfth century is open to visitors.

The 'Gerontius' stained-glass window near the north door was erected to the memory of Sir Edward Elgar. It depicts scenes from the composer's choral masterpiece 'The Dream of Gerontius' which was given its first successful British performance in the cathedral in 1902.

Leaving the Cathedral pass the war memorial to men of Worcestershire who died in the South African Campaign, 1899-1902, in front of which is a fine Victorian letter box.

Statue of Sir Edward Elgar

If you are using public transport go forward along the pedestrianised High Street, passing the statue of Sir Edward Elgar on your right and soon, on your left, the fine Guildhall. Turn left along Angel Street to return to Crowngate or continue forward for Worcester Foregate station.

For the car park turn left along Deansgate to reach a tower and spire, all that remains of St Andrew's Church.

St Andrew's Church *once had five bells, but four were sold in 1870. The medieval tenor bell (about 20 cwt) still hangs in the old frame. As a Jubilee project the City Council installed a clock that strikes the hours and so, after having been silent for about 100 years, this bell can be heard once again.*

The exceptionally slender spire, 75 metres high, is reputed to be the tallest in the country and is known as "The Glover's Needle" in recognition of the numerous craftsmen and their families who lived in the parish. In the eighteenth and nineteenth centuries Worcester specialised in glove-making.

Just before the Glover's Needle turn left to regain Kleeve Walk for a short walk back to Worcester Bridge.

5

Elgar's Birthplace

Upper Broadheath

Special Feature: Elgar's birthplace museum and Elgar Centre.

Distance: A: 9.5km/6 miles; B: 6.25km/4 miles.
Start: Elgar Centre (GR808557). *Open daily 11.00am – 5.00pm Last admission 4.15. Closed for about a month around Christmas and the New Year.*
Maps: Explorer 204; Landranger 150.
Car Parking: Car park by the Elgar Birthplace Museum, Crown Road East, Upper Broadheath (GR808557).
Public Transport: Service 41 from Worcester to Dines Green. This adds about 2 miles/3.2km but provides a pleasant bridleway walk. Leave the bus in Tudor Way, immediately after the bus turns into it from Drake Avenue, and then follow the instructions in the box on page 44.
Terrain: Fairly level with no difficult ascents. Mostly field paths and quiet lanes with some fine views of the Malverns.
Refreshments: The Plough near the birthplace museum, the Fox Inn at Bransford Bridge.

The Pubs

The Plough: A welcoming and conveniently placed pub with a wide menu of meals and snacks and two good cask ales.
The Fox Inn: Obviously, from the oak beams, a very old inn though I was not able to get any of its history. Much extended to provide restaurant facilities. A couple of cask ales.

From the Elgar Centre walk past The Plough on your right and after about 50 metres go left along a driveway which swings left to approach a house. At the end of a conifer hedge on the right turn right through a gate into a field. Walk with a hedge on the right to go through a gate, continue forward to reach a high conifer hedge on your right, then go diagonally left to cross a stile in a fence ahead. Continue to cross another stile in the far left corner of the field. Here pass a stone post and turn left to walk between farm buildings, going through several gates, some of which may be open. Continue along a farm track for about 100 metres to approach another gate; here swing left through yet another farm gate, then swing right and go forward on a good track. You now have a fine view of the Malverns ahead. *I wonder if this was one of the infant Elgar's first views of the hills that he grew to love so much?*

Follow the track through more gates until it comes to an end where a gate takes you into a field. Now continue forward with a hedge on the right to go through another gate that leads you onto a road opposite a Garden Centre & Restaurant. Go right for a few metres and then cross the road and a stile just to the left of the Centre. Follow a green lane hedged on both sides, soon crossing a wooded stream to enter a field with a hedge and fence on the right. Go through a gate and walk with a hedge on the left and a fence on the right, very shortly crossing a stile and continuing with the hedge on the left. Follow the hedge as it turns right and then, as it starts to turn right again, cross a stile on the left and descend to Lower Howsen Farm.

Here the A and B walks separate. For the longer A walk continue reading from ☆ on page 42.

Following the shorter walk B, turn left past the first building to pass barns on the right and then, approaching a gate ahead, turn right to enter a field through a gate. From here the right of way, as indicated by a waymark and the OS map, goes diagonally left. However, there was not, when I was last here, a stile in the fence ahead so it proved necessary to go straight forward

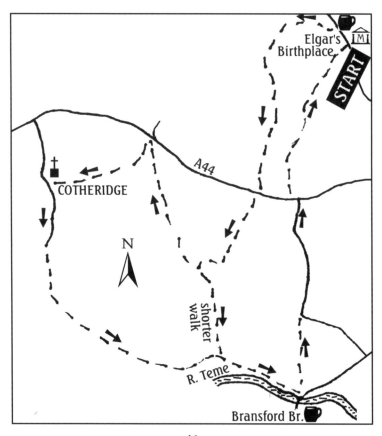

and through a gate. Then go diagonally left aiming to the left of two large willows ahead. Here meet a footbridge: don't cross it but turn left to re-join walk A. Now continue from ✸ on page 43.

✩ Turn right past the first building and walk with the farmhouse and staddlestones on your left. Go through a large wooden gate and continue along tarmac past farm buildings, swinging right, then left and ascending, then right to descend to a stream. About 30 metres beyond the stream cross a stile on the left and go slightly right passing a pool on the left and cross a stile in the fence ahead into another field.

We shall soon leave this field by a footbridge which, although not yet visible, is diagonally left and between two large willows in the hedge on the left. However, keeping to the right of way go forward to the corner of the field to the right of a bungalow, then turn back to walk parallel to the hedge on the right to reach and cross this footbridge. *As a good rambler you always, of course, keep to rights of way!*

Having crossed the footbridge go half right with a fence on your right. Reaching the end of the field (a mass of buttercups in May) reach a road with Cotheridge Parish Church of St Leonard on the corner on the right. St Leonard is the patron saint of prisoners.

__Cotheridge Parish Church__. Don't miss the opportunity to visit this most interesting church. Entering through the porch note the old funeral bier. The chancel and the nave have a partition wall between them containing a Norman arch and were built early in the twelfth century. The south windows date from the time of the Magna Carta. The timber bell tower was built from oak beams in cruk fashion just before the first Church of England prayer book was published in

Cotheridge Church

1548. Of especial interest in the chancel are some glazed floor tiles from the fourteenth and fifteenth centuries. One shows an elephant which must have seemed almost a mythical beast to parishioners in those times! Others carry the arms of the Berkeley family and of the Throckmorton family. The latter were fanatical papists and organised a plot to assassinate Queen Elizabeth I. The plot was, of course, discovered and it was Throckmorton who lost his life.

After leaving the church turn left along a lane with a good view of North Hill ahead. At the end of the lane pass a farm and go forward through a gate; cross a farm track and go across the field to reach a stile at the right-hand end of a section of the hedge straight ahead. Cross this and turn left to walk with a hedge on your left. When, after almost a 100 metres, you reach a farm gate on your left swing half right, aiming for a stile at the right-hand end of a line of trees and bushes ahead.

After crossing the stile you should, to follow the right of way, go through a gate on the right and walk at a slight angle to the fence on your left and cross a stile about 30 metres to the right of the left-hand end of the fence ahead. However, if crops make this difficult it may be easier not to go through the gate but to continue with the fence on your right (and a hedge on your left), then go through a gate and turn right for about 30 metres to reach the stile on the right of way. (*There have been a number of changes here since I first designed this walk and it looks as though this might be the preferred route.*)

Now, having crossed, or with your back to, the stile go straight forward to cross another stile, continue through a gate and walk with a hedge on your left. At the end of the field cross a footbridge and turn right.

❀ *B walkers join here.*

Go through a gate and continue forward across the field ahead. At the far right-hand corner of the field go through a gate and walk with the River Teme on the right to approach a road and reach a wooden hut.

If you wish to visit the Fox Inn, continue forward to leave the field by a kissing-gate. Turn right and cross Bransford Bridge.

With your back to the wooden hut go forward across the field, aiming for a stile that is about 40 metres to the left of the leftmost of two trees in the boundary ahead. *Growing crops once forced me to follow tractor tracks to reach this.* Cross the stile and turn left as waymarked. Follow round the sides of this field to reach and cross a footbridge and a stile in the far left-hand corner. Walk up the steep field, looking behind for a good view of the Malverns, cross a stile in the far left-hand corner of the field and continue forward along Otherton Lane to reach the main road. Cross this carefully and turn left for a few metres, then turn right to cross a rough area and reach a hidden and easily missed stile just to the right of a large tree. A footpath sign points to Broadheath.

Now, keeping the field boundary and a stream on your left, walk through four fields (more buttercups), a white house appearing at the top left corner of the fourth field. Cross a stile in this corner and turn left for about 50 metres to reach Elgar's birthplace museum on the right. Note the punning notice 'PLEASE BOULT THE GATE' (The conductor Sir Adrian Boult was a great interpreter of Elgar). Just inside the gate, on the left, is a stone marking the grave of two of Elgar's favourite dogs.

Elgar's Birthplace

Route from Dines Green

From the Tudor Way bus stop in Dines Green walk back along Tudor Way, passing Drake Avenue on the right. Turn left along Oldbury Road and at the end of the tarmac, where there is a cattle-grid on the right, go forward between fences along a signed public bridleway. If you look back as the bridleway ascends you will get a view of Worcester with the Cathedral and the tall elegant spire of the Glover's Needle (see p. 39) standing out prominently. To the right is the long line of the Cotswolds. Pass Oldbury Farm on the right, go through a gate and along a driveway leading to Oldbury Grange. Go through another gate, turn left (*remember this turn for your return*) and follow the bridleway to reach the start of the walk. Approaching a road, Elgar's Birthplace is on the left and the Elgar Museum on the right. The Plough Inn is on the road, a short distance to the right.

6

British Camp and Elgar's Grave

Malvern

Special Features: British Camp, Elgar's grave, Little Malvern Court, Little Malvern Priory.

Distance: 10 km/6¼ miles.
Start: British Camp (GR763403).
Maps: Explorer 190; Landranger 150.
Car Parking: British Camp car park (GR763403).
Public Transport: Bus service 675 Malvern-British Camp-Ledbury.
Terrain: Strenuous, with some steep ascents and descents, excellent views, fine woodland. Some tarmac, mostly quiet lanes. About 750 metres of main road but a good pavement.
Refreshments: Malvern Hills Hotel, British Camp.

The Pub
Malvern Hills Hotel, British Camp
A welcoming hotel, popular with walkers. Good food and five cask ales including several local brews.

From the British Camp car park pass the Herefordshire Beacon plaque (having first studied it) that is immediately on the right as you enter the car park and walk up the steeply ascending tarmac and stepped path, turning right, then left after a few metres. Continue, ignoring all paths off, until you reach the highest point where the surfacing ends. As you ascend you will cross the ditches that comprise the fortifications of the British Camp earthworks, dating back to the second century BC. *From the highest point, on a clear day, there are superb views all around, west across Herefordshire, east across Worcestershire and taking in the Clee Hills, the South Shropshire Hills, the Brecon Beacons and the Cotswolds. To the south can be seen the obelisk in Eastnor Park erected in 1812.*

This area was particularly loved by Sir Edward Elgar who was inspired by it to write his oratorio Caractacus, based on the British chieftain who may have been responsible for the earthworks.

Continue walking south, keeping to the high ground, the well-used stony track eventually giving way to grass. To the left the reservoir that we shall pass on the way back can soon be seen. Descend steeply on a stone surfaced path (*this can be treacherous after rain*) and then, at an indicator pillar (one of many erected by the Malvern Hills Conservators) turn right (signed Giant's Cave and Pink Cottage). You very soon pass, on the left, a

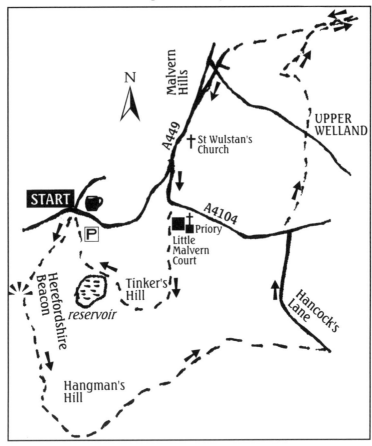

cave cut into the rock, known both as Clutter's Cave and the Giant's Cave (but presumably a rather small giant!), the origin of which is unknown.

Stay on the well-trodden track, ignoring paths off, and passing through woodland. When you meet a junction of paths, where on the left there is a stone marker signed Hangman's Hill and Broad Down, bear right to continue along the main track, soon passing another junction of paths where you bear slightly left and continue to descend. After about 200 metres reach a track on the left and turn sharp left to walk along this. Pass a house on the right and continue ahead along a path through bracken which ascends and then descends steeply through woodland to meet another path near to power lines. Go forward to walk under the power lines, cross a track and walk with a hedge and fence on your right. As you proceed down the field it widens out. In its far left-hand corner cross a stile, turn right and walk beside a wire fence on your right until you reach a wicket gate.

Go through the gate and walk along an enclosed path, that can be rather muddy. This leads to more open country where you continue on the

A view of the Malverns

same bearing, eventually joining a track coming in from the right. Cross a stream to reach a gated road and turn left along this. As the road swings right and the trees disappear on the left there is now a good view of the Malverns and the remains of Malvern Priory on the left. Reaching a main road turn left along this for a few metres, cross it and take a lane on the right signed Mayalls Farm. Bear left past the farm and when you meet a Y-junction take the right fork. After passing houses reach a road, now in Upper Welland: here turn right for a few metres and then go left along a No Through Road (Chase Road).

At the end of Chase Road take a waymarked path to the right of a gate and cross a stile after a few metres. Continue along this enclosed path, crossing another stile and soon emerging onto a road (Assarts Lane). Cross this and continue forward along a bridleway which very shortly swings right by a gas installation. After about 450 metres leave the path through a gate to enter a field, where there is a multiplicity of waymarks, and turn sharp left and walk with a hedge on your left, initially parallel to the path you have just left. Continue through a second field, go through a waymarked gate and follow a delightful path along the edge of woodland, bordered with lots of wild flowers in the spring. At the end of this turn left along a lane and reaching a crossroads continue straight ahead up Kings Road to reach and turn left along the A449.

There is now some main road walking, but there is a substantial pavement – and a good view of the Cotswolds to the left. After about 200 metres turn left along the driveway which takes you down to St Wulstan's Church. Go round to the back of the church, then forward to reach Elgar's grave just before a gate. Now return to the road and continue along it for

47

about 175 metres to reach a junction. Here turn left along the A4104. There is a good view on the left of the Worcestershire countryside with soon, diagonally left ahead, Little Malvern Priory nestling in the trees.

Little Malvern Court. Almost at the bottom of the hill on the right is Little Malvern Court, the Court and its magnificent gardens being open to the public from mid-April to mid-July, Weds/Thurs afternoons (there is an admission charge). Next to the Court is **Little Malvern Priory** *open daily. Parts of this date back to the twelfth century. During the Civil War Cromwell's troops were responsible for the loss of its stained glass windows and other damage, but there is still much to see.*

Elgar's Grave

Now go back a little way up the hill and take the first turning on your left, soon passing on the left the attractive garden of Little Malvern Court with two lakes and bounded by some fine topiary. Past the garden continue for about 250 metres to reach a stile beside a gate with a fine yew tree on the right. Cross the stile and walk diagonally left across the field towards woodland. This takes you on to an old grassy track (that may not be very apparent) that passes to the right of a large lime tree and reaches an iron gate to the left of a cattle trough (*not the gate that is directly forward from the stile*).

Go through the gate onto a bridlepath that takes you up through Tinker's Wood, ascending to reach a Y-junction of paths. Continue straight forward to reach a green metal fence that encloses the dam of the reservoir that we shall soon meet and which provides some of Malvern's water supply. Pass the reservoir where ahead is a good view of the Herefordshire Beacon that formed the first part of the walk. Follow the surfaced lane to return to the starting point of the walk in the car park.

7

This, That and T'other

Knightwick

Special Features: The Talbot Inn and Teme Valley Brewery.

Distance: 14km/8¾ miles. This is a figure of eight walk, divided into two sections, A: 8km/5 miles, B: 6 km/3¾ miles.
Start: Knightwick A44 at GR732558.
Maps: Explorer 204; Landranger 150.
Car Parking: In a side road off the A44 at Knightwick, GR732558.
Public Transport: Bus service 420 Worcester/Hereford. Alight at Knightwick.
Terrain: Hilly, especially on section B where there are some steep climbs.
Refreshments: The Talbot Inn, Knightwick.

The Pub

The Talbot Inn (GBG)
This fourteenth century tavern and coaching inn (with accommodation) is a delight and this figure of eight walk gives you two opportunities to visit it (there is a reasonable bus service from Worcester!). It has an enviable reputation for its food, many of the ingredients coming from the owners' farm and organic garden. The buildings behind the pub house a small brewery, Teme Valley Brewery, producing some fine cask ales with the intriguing names of This, That, T'other and Wot, most of the hops coming from the nearby Lulsley Court Estate, passed on the A walk. Bar snacks and meals in the pub, lunchtimes and evenings.
Near to the Talbot locally produced wine can be bought (Fridays 4.30-7.00 pm; Saturdays 11.00 am – 6.00 pm; Sundays 11.00 am – 3.00 pm.

A walk

Leave the A44 on its south side, go forward a few metres on a minor road and almost immediately turn left along the road signed Lulsley and Alfrick. Follow this for about a kilometre/0.6 mile. Reaching woodland the road rises and almost at the highest point passes the remains of an old railway bridge. A few metres beyond this take the signed bridleway on the right (Worcestershire Way) and follow the rising stony path. Eventually passing through a gate you get some attractive views to the left. Pass through two more gates to enter a field, now walking with a wood on the right. Continue through a second field, passing a stile and woodland on the right, an attractive view of the Malverns soon appearing on the left.

Go through a pair of gates when there is now woodland on the left and more pleasant views on the right. Pass through yet another pair of gates and after about 600 metres (and having passed a waymark post and stile on the right) the path swings slightly left and passes under power lines. After another few metres reach a waymark post and here turn very sharp left, now leaving the Worcestershire Way, and follow the grassy path to join a drive-way along which you walk towards a house.

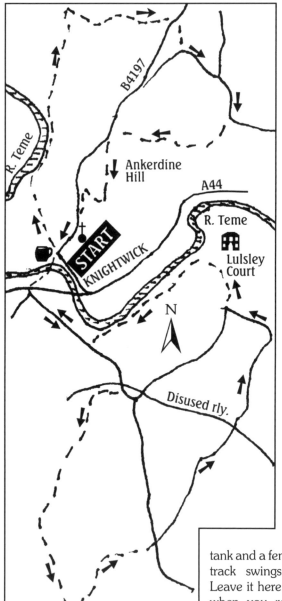

Just before reaching the garden of the house go right along a descending path into the trees. Very soon cross a stile and continue to descend through Ravenhill Wood. After going through a rather muddy area reach a track coming in from the left and turn right along it. The wood-land here is quite delightful.

When you reach a tank and a fence on the left the main track swings left and descends. Leave it here and go forward, then when you reach the end of the woodland cross a stile, passing a house on the right, to emerge onto a road. Cross this, go a few metres left and then turn right along a lane, passing a post-box and a pool on the right. Very shortly, at Ravenshills Green on the right, note an old cider press in front of a wooden building. Follow this pleasant quiet lane for about 1.5 km, en route passing over the line of the disused railway, a bridge of which was encountered earlier. After passing through a delightful sunken tree-lined section and meeting a track coming in from the right, the lane swings sharp left. Continue for about another 400 metres when the road again swings sharp left. Here leave the road and go forward for a few metres towards a telegraph post, then turn right through gates and descend past Colles Place, following the surfaced track as it swings left past a hop-field.

Pass on the right the timber-framed Lulsley Court, admiring its delightful gardens and swinging round left to reach a gate beside modern housing. Here turn left to ascend steps and go through a gate, then turn right to walk beside a fence. Go through a gate and then half right across a field, with a fine view of Ankerdine Hill ahead (walked on the other loop of this walk), to a gap in the hedge in the far corner. Here cross a stile beside a gate and bear left to walk with a hedge and fence on your left and the River Teme across to the right. To avoid boggy patches in the field keep up high, close to the fence.

Leave the field by a stile and with Osebury Rock on the left follow the pleasant riverside path, then cross another stile into a field. *To the sides of the path in early May were masses of wild garlic flowers.* Go half left across the field and leave it by a stile beside a gate, joining the road along which you walked at the start of the walk. Turn right along this to reach your starting point. You now have the option of continuing on Walk B (steeper hills than there have been on this section!). However don't miss The Talbot and to reach this just follow the first part of Walk B.

The Talbot

51

B Walk

Leave the A44 on its northern side and walk along the 'No Through Road' (signed Worcestershire Way) passing a doctor's surgery. Cross a substantial footbridge (the old coach road) over the River Teme and reach the Talbot Inn. Immediately past the inn turn left along tarmac. On the left, behind a row of conifers, is a hop-field and on the right a nursery. Ahead you may just make out the tops of two oast-houses. When you reach these walk to the right of them through a farmyard (Ankerdine Farm). The track now swings right passing alongside power cables. The River Teme is over to the left and you are soon walking alongside this.

After crossing a stile beside a gate leave the river, which meanders off to the left, and swing right towards Horsham Farm which can be seen ahead. Cross two stiles (or through the adjacent gates) and just before reaching the farm turn sharp right and walk with a hedge and fence on the left. After crossing a stile beside a gate start to climb and cross another stile. Through a gap in the hedge on the left you may see two more oast-houses in the distance.

Cross another stile beside a gate and walk straight forward across the field through bracken, ascending steeply and passing under power lines (multi-waymarked power pole at a crossing path) with Hay Wood on the right. Cross a waymarked stile into Tinkers Coppice and follow the meandering path, yellow painted waymarks (rather weathered) marking out the route.

Reaching a road turn left along this for about 50 metres, then take a waymarked path on the right with a hedge and driveway on the left. This leads to a narrow lane along which you turn left and follow it as it descends between high hedges. Reaching a T-junction turn right – we are now joined by the Worcestershire Way.

Pass the nicely named Hawksnest Farm and look out for a good view of the Malverns ahead. About 200 metres past the farm the road swings sharply left but here turn right along a waymarked Worcestershire Way path, going through a gate. Now walk with a hedge and soon a wood on the left. Keep close to the hedge and just before the edge of the wood swings away to the left meet a Worcestershire Way waymark post. Continue ahead passing a gate to your left and descend with a fence on the left. Follow the fence round along the edge of the wood ahead to reach a waymark post and a stile leading into the wood (about 100 metres from the left-hand edge of the field).

Cross the stile and a footbridge to ascend, turning right at a T-junction and waymark post. This section is inclined to be quite muddy. At a Y-junction turn left, still following the Worcestershire Way. The path now becomes drier and meanders around in the wood, with periodic reassurances from Worcestershire Way waymarks, and climbs, quite steeply at times. Leave the wood by a stile and walk up a field towards a gate, passing an interestingly shaped house. Leave the field by a kissing gate, go forward a few metres and then left along a track, passing The Laurels on the left and Ankerdine Cottage on the right.

On meeting a waymarked Y-junction continue forward along the Worcestershire Way (and the Fox Trail) ascending along a brick track, very shortly passing a viewpoint. Follow the broad track for about 200 metres, going through a white gate, passing en route a path on the right and another fine viewpoint reached by steps, to reach a house. Continue past this for a few metres, then turn right to descend steps. Continue your descent along the meandering path following the Worcestershire Way waymarks and soon leaving the Fox Trail, eventually descending steps to reach a road.

You have been walking on Ankerdine Hill and as you leave the woodland look back at the County Council information notice about woodlands.

Old cider press at The Talbot

Turn left along the road and follow it down for (more?) welcome refreshment at The Talbot. Entering the village pass Knightwick Church and note the flood level mark by the door. The Teme Valley Brewery and Old School Wines are at the rear of the inn. In The Talbot garden, opposite the inn, look for the old cider press.

Recross the bridge over the Teme and retrace your steps towards the A44 and your starting point.

8

Jewels of the Cotswolds

Broadway and Bretforton

Special Features: The Fleece Inn, Bretforton (walks A and B); Saintbury Church, Willersey (walks A and C); Broadway with its many fine Cotswold buildings (walks A and B).

Distance: A: 16 km/10 miles; B: 10.5 km/6¾ miles; C: 8 km/5 miles.
Start: Walks A and C: Broadway, The Swan Inn (GR094376); Walk B: Willersey (GR088377).
Maps: Explorer 205 & OL45; Landranger 150.
Car Parking: Walks A and C; Childswickham Road, Broadway, off the B4632 (GR088377). From the car park walk back along Childswickham Road, at the T-junction turn left, then at the next T-junction turn right to reach the Swan Inn on the left as you enter the village.
Walk B: Willersey, car park by the Village Hall, along a driveway opposite the Bell Inn (GR104395).
.**Public Transport:** Rail and bus services to Evesham, then 559 bus service to Broadway (leave the bus at the Swan Inn) or Willersey (leave the bus at the village pond, opposite the Bell Inn).
Terrain: A fairly vigorous ascent on the return stretch of walks A and C but otherwise easy walking, mostly along fieldpaths, with some quiet lanes.
Refreshments: Pubs in Bretforton and Willersey, pubs and other refreshment opportunities in Broadway.
More information about Broadway and its buildings can be obtained from the Tourist Information Office. This is in the Cotswold Court shopping arcade, near the start of the walk and close to the war memorial.

The Pubs

The Fleece Inn, Bretforton
Sadly, this wonderful country pub was seriously damaged by fire in 2004. Most of the damage was confined to the upper floors and it is being restored. It is owned by, and had been beautifully preserved by, the National Trust. Four centuries old, half-timbered and roofed with stone tiles, it was originally a farmhouse and became an inn in 1848. It was passed to the National Trust in 1977, furniture and all, on condition that it would be left essentially unchanged. The grandest part of the pub was the Pewter Room, originally the farm kitchen, and taking its name from the splendid 48 piece pewter dinner service that is thought to date back to the Civil War when it replaced the family silver that had been seized and melted down.

Thankfully this was rescued from the fire.Good food and several cask ales, including local brews, and traditional cider.

The Crown and Trumpet, Church Street, Broadway. **(GBG)**
A seventeenth century inn of Cotswold stone, popular with locals, tourists and walkers, being on both the Cotswold and Donnington Ways. The interior is very comfortable with oak beams, open fires, good food and some fine cask ales, one of which, Stanway Cotteswold Gold, is brewed specially for this pub.

The Bell Inn, Willersey
A seventeenth century building of Cotswold stone, overlooking the village green and duck pond. Good food and cask ales.

The New Inn, Willersey
This looks very promising (it is a Donnington's pub) but I was not able to visit it.

A and C walks (for the B walk go to page 62.)

Walk to the left of the Swan Inn on Broadway High Street passing a car parking area. Turn right along Back Lane, then left along Walnut Close and follow this round until just past metal gates on the right, then turn right to walk in front of a pair of thatched cottages along a signed footpath. Go through a wicket gate (right) and turn left along a track between fields. When the track swings slightly to the left go through a wicket gate and follow a path, initially parallel to the track, and passing houses on the right. On leaving the houses cross a footbridge and go straight ahead across a field. Cross a stile and walk with a fence on the right, then leave the fence to walk briefly with a remains of a hedge on the left. Continue the same bearing, soon being joined by a hedge on the right.

When the hedge ends at a corner continue forward to reach a footbridge about 30 metres to the left of the far right corner of the field. Cross this and then bear left to cross a stile and pass under the main road. Cross another stile and turn right, then left to walk with a stream on the right. At the end of a row of willows cross a footbridge on the right and walk with the stream now on the left. Pass a footpath on the right, the stream here going into a culvert. Continue forward to join another path along which you turn right for just a few metres, then turn left to rejoin the stream and cross a stile.

Continue beside the stream, cross another stile to walk with a fence on the right and enter a field through an iron gate. Go diagonally right to a wicket gate, walking across ridge and furrow and leave the field by a stile to reach a road.

Here the A and C walks separate. For the longer walk A cross the road and now continue reading from ✪ *on page 56.*

Continuing walk C turn right along the road and follow it for just over half a mile/1 km to reach a crossroads. En route you cross a bridge over a

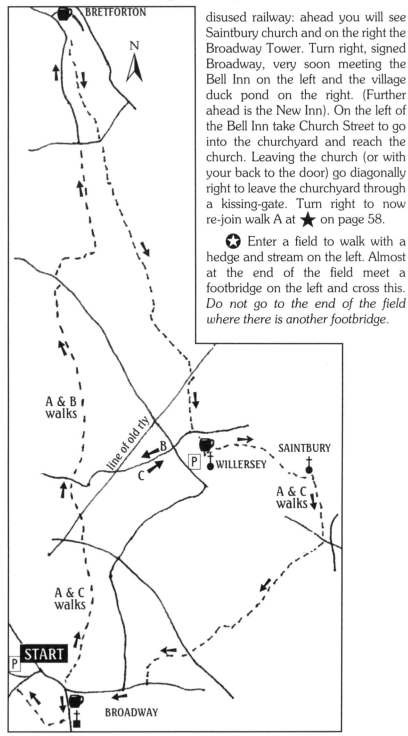

disused railway: ahead you will see Saintbury church and on the right the Broadway Tower. Turn right, signed Broadway, very soon meeting the Bell Inn on the left and the village duck pond on the right. (Further ahead is the New Inn). On the left of the Bell Inn take Church Street to go into the churchyard and reach the church. Leaving the church (or with your back to the door) go diagonally right to leave the churchyard through a kissing-gate. Turn right to now re-join walk A at ★ on page 58.

✪ Enter a field to walk with a hedge and stream on the left. Almost at the end of the field meet a footbridge on the left and cross this. *Do not go to the end of the field where there is another footbridge.*

Over the footbridge cross a stile and turn right to walk with the stream on the right. Although the paths are well waymarked in this area this particular one was not marked when I was last here. Now continue beside the stream, keeping it on your right, for about 1.5 km (just under a mile) going through six fields and en route crossing two footbridges and a tarmac track leading to Downrip Farm.

When, in the sixth field you meet an electric fence cross a stile to walk with the fence on your left. About 50 metres before the end of the field go right to cross the stream over a culvert and go diagonally left, passing to the right of a large oak and crossing pronounced ridge and furrow to reach a gate and join Badsey Lane. Walk left along this for about 40 metres and then turn right along a tarmac bridleway. Follow this as it turns right across a cattle grid, pass to the right of Willersey Barn (keep the fence on your left) and go through a gate beside a cattle grid. Turn left to continue along the bridleway and, on reaching a road T-junction, go forward to Bretforton, Bretforton Church tower soon appearing ahead. Just past a 30 sign the road swings left: here the return route is over a stile to the right but to reach the Fleece Inn continue forward along the road (Back Lane). Just before reaching a seat and a grassed area turn right over a stream, passing stone cottages. Reaching the church swing round to the right to the Fleece Inn which is somewhat hidden behind trees.

After refreshment retrace your steps to cross the stream and turn left along Back Lane. When the lane swings right go forward across a stile and walk with a stream on the left. The stream meanders away left and then swings back where you join it again to walk through a gap at the left-hand end of a fence, shortly passing a similar gap at another fence. Now follow

The Fleece Inn (before the fire).

beside the meandering and wooded stream for about 2km/1¼ miles. There has been considerable hedge removal here so I won't list how many fields you pass through in case more disappear. You will, however, cross a number of stiles, a footbridge, a tarmac driveway into a farm, and go through a gate and several hedge gaps, good views of the Cotswolds opening up ahead.

About 35 metres before the field boundary swings right, turn left to cross the stream (heading towards a new plantation), then immediately turn right and then left around the corner of the field. After about 50 metres cross a footbridge on the right across the stream. Turn left and walk with a hedge on the left, cross a footbridge and walk with hedge and young woodland on the left. Cross a stile and go across a field, then ascend a slope to cross a dismantled railway (the old Gloucestershire and Warwickshire Railway line). Then turn right for about 50 metres to reach a waymark post and here turn left.

Go straight forward across the field aiming towards the tower of Willersey church. Pass a waymark on a corner post, walk to the left of a pear tree (with a good crop in late October) and cross a stile (*possibly now redundant because on my last visit there was a hedge gap beside it*) to continue forward towards Willersey church, passing through prominent ridge and furrow. Leave the field through a kissing gate to join a road. Go left along this for a few metres, then right through another kissing gate, and with a fence, then a wall, on the right aim once again for the church and reach a kissing gate leading into the churchyard.

★ *Here A walkers turn left to walk beside the churchyard (but do first visit the church), being joined by C walkers. B walkers continue reading from* ❀ *on page 62.*

The Church of St Peter. *This beautiful cruciform church contains traces of Saxon, Norman and Early English architectural styles and was enlarged in the fourteenth and fifteenth centuries by the abbots of Evesham who lived in Willersey Manor House. It has, unusually for its age, a central bell tower with six bells. These had been recast in 1712 from three earlier bells and were first rung as a thanksgiving for the end of the War of the Spanish Succession (1701-1714). The War was the first major engagement of English forces on the European continent beyond French coastal areas. It was an enormous expense and had become increasingly unpopular in England.*

The tower carries some immense gargoyles. The tub font is early Norman and is thought to have been preserved from destruction by the Puritans by being hidden in the rectory garden. The west window contains some fragments of medieval glass. In the chancel look along the top of the wall for 'The Angels of the Passion', so called because they contain the symbols of Christ's Crucifixion in their hands. The south window here is nineteenth century and forms a remarkable memorial to a family lost at sea.

More information can be found in a descriptive leaflet available in the church.

We are now on the Donnington Way that we shall follow for a while. This is a 62 mile walk linking pubs of the Donnington Brewery. Ahead Saintbury Church comes into view – our next objective. Cross a stile and a stone footbridge to walk with a hedge on the left for a few metres and then cross two stiles on the left. Walk with a hedge on the right for about 50 metres and then cross a stile on the right to go diagonally left, passing to the left of a power pole. Cross a stream and two more stiles, then walk up a field with a hedge and fence on the left, passing a stile on the left. Cross another stile and continue to ascend, soon walking beside a wooden fence and following it as in turns left. Pass some attractive stone cottages and then cross a stile to reach a gate leading into the churchyard and ascend steps to the church.

Saintbury Church

Saintbury Church. *The church of St Nicholas is Norman and later, but a Saxon church originally stood on the site and some fragments of it remain. Most notably is a remarkable Anglo-Saxon mass dial (a primitive sundial) situated on the south wall above a blocked Norman doorway. The elegant spire houses six bells and there is a Queen Anne vaulted roof. In the south transept there is a strange octagonal stone known as the 'pre-Christian altar' and believed to pre-date the Saxon church. In the north transept there is another large stone underneath a Jacobean table and it is thought that this may have been used as an altar in medieval times. On the south side is a Sheila-na-gig, a goddess of fertility in British Celtic mythology, portrayed as a female demon to ward off evil. From the churchyard you have a fine view over the Vale of Evesham.*

This spot has an air of mystery about it, perhaps reflecting its history, and maybe because a 'ley line' passes through the eastern end of the church. The concept of 'ley lines' is due to Alfred Watkins who, in 1921, put forward the theory that ancient sites around Britain, including stone circles, standing stones, long barrows, cairns, burial mounds and churches were aligned along straight lines. Archeologists are inclined to think that these alignments are due to nothing more than coincidence, but the concept has some firm believers.

Leave the churchyard by a gate in the south-east corner, go forward through a kissing-gate and ascend a zigzag path through woodland. This path is not too well defined in places so you may sometimes have to do a bit of guesswork. However, as long as you keep ascending you will eventually leave the wood through a kissing-gate. Then walk forward through a large field with a hedge and trees on the left, aiming for the far right-hand corner of the field.

Cross a stone stile a little to the right of that corner, descend steps, cross a lane and follow a bridleway, which can be rather muddy in places. On the right, as you turn off, there is a good view of Bredon Hill and the Malverns. The bridleway leads along the edge of a golf course and a sign warns you to beware of golf balls. However, since there are trees between the bridleway and the golf course it is impossible to see any golfers and whether a ball might be coming your way. Perhaps a hard hat is called for! The bridleway soon leaves the hedge and emerges onto the edge of the course, but then returns between hedges.

After swinging left the bridleway emerges again into the golf course which you leave through a gap beside a gate on the right. Descend towards tarmac, cross this, go through a gate and continue to descend, walking to the left of an oak, then to the right of another where there is also a waymark post. Ahead you have a good view of Broadway. Swing left, then right, soon passing another waymark post, and aim for a gate in the woodland ahead. Go through the gate and walk between mature woodland on the left and a younger section on the right. Go through a small wooden gate and descend on a clear path towards a road. Go through two more gates and pass under the road.

Emerging from the underpass fork right, cross a stile beside a gate and walk briefly along a track to approach a stile beside a gate. Don't cross it but cross a footbridge on the left and follow an enclosed path with a field on the right. *A waymark on that stile indicates that the right of way goes along the side of the field but this path is well used and appears to be the preferred route.* Soon turn left and go through a kissing gate onto a road. Turn right along this, then after a few metres turn left. At a T-junction turn right, then just past Orchard Avenue on the right take a waymarked path on the left. Reaching Broadway High Street turn right, passing some beautiful old cottages on the left.

Broadway is a delightful village with many old buildings constructed from the local limestone. You can obtain an interesting guide from the Tourist Information Office that details many of these and I have used this to pick out a few that we shall now be passing.

Cross Leamington Road where at the corner you will see Priors Manse, built around 1320 and one of the oldest buildings in the town. On the opposite side of the road is Tudor House, built 1659-60, with its impressive clock. Once an inn, it now houses an antiques gallery. Continuing along the High Street pass the Horse and Hound and more fine buildings, mostly built from local sandstone in the seventeenth and eighteenth centuries.

Soon pass Picton House (opposite the HSBC bank) built in 1700 and now an art gallery. It was once an inn when Broadway was an important coaching stop with thirty-three inns. Note the fine gateposts that may have come from Broadway Court, demolished in 1773. Look out in front of Picton House for the stone inscribed 'Start of two horses here'– this was originally on the nearby Fish Hill and served as a reminder to coachmen that extra horses were needed for the steep climb.

Ahead, on the right, is the impressive Lygon (pronounced *Liggon*)Arms Hotel.

Bus travellers will find the stop for Evesham opposite the Lygon Arms.

The Lygon Arms. *The first recorded date in the history of this hotel (then the White Hart Inn) is 1532, although there are indications that it is much older. The fine front doorway dates from the sixteenth century.*

The wool trade, which played an important part in the economy of the Cotswolds in the fifteenth and sixteenth centuries, created a need for accommodation, such as the White Hart Inn, for merchants who frequently travelled between the prosperous wool towns of Broadway and Chipping Campden. In the eighteenth century the inn became an important staging post for coaches travelling through Broadway along the main road from London to Wales, when the journey between Worcester and London took seventeen hours.

Charles I met his supporters here, and Oliver Cromwell stayed at the inn on 2 September 1651, the night before the Battle of Worcester.

In 1820, General William Lygon, who had served under Wellington at the Battle of Waterloo, bought the estate on which the inn stood, for £1,580. Before his death, Lygon promoted his butler, Charles Drury, to be manager, and it was he who renamed the White Hart Inn as The Lygon Arms.

Cross the road and turn right to pass the Broadway Hotel.

To return directly to the car park continue past Church Street, turn left along the B4632, then right along Childswickham Road. Alternatively, for refreshment at the Crown and Trumpet and/or to use footpaths to reach the car park turn into Church Street, passing three almshouses, two of which were built around 1600, with their delightful gardens. Then, very shortly, reach the Crown and Trumpet.

For the footpaths to the car park continue past the Crown and Trumpet for about 100 metres and take a Cotswold Way footpath on the right. Go through a kissing-gate and continue forward to cross a footbridge and here turn right (now leaving the Cotswold Way) to walk beside a stream, soon crossing another footbridge. After crossing another stile walk through some attractive gardens to reach the B4632, turn right along this, then, after about 100 metres, turn left along Childswickham Road to the car park.

B walk

Leave the car park in Willersey, walk up to the Bell Inn and turn left along the road, passing the village duck pond. Reaching a crossroads turn left along Collin Lane Follow the lane for just over half a mile/1 km and about 100 metres after the road swings sharp right meet footpath waymarks on left and right. Here take the path on the right and now join the A walk at ✪ on page 56.

✿ Go into the churchyard, then from the church follow a flagged path to leave the churchyard and walk along Church Street. Reach a T-junction and here turn left by the Bell Inn for the car park on the right.

9

'My Kingdom for a Horse'

Bosworth Field

Special Features: Bosworth Battlefield, The Ashby Canal, The Battlefield Line.

Distance: A: 13 km/8 miles; B: 8 km/5 miles; C: 10.5 km/6½ miles.
Start: Bosworth Battlefield Visitor Centre (GR403001).
Maps: Explorer 232, 233; Landranger 140.
Car Parking: Bosworth Battlefield Visitor Centre car park (GR403001).
Public Transport: Bus service 153 from Leicester to Market Bosworth. Start reading from ✪ on page 65.
Terrain: Some undulations but nothing difficult. Field paths, canalside and minor roads. One hill (Ambion Hill) optional.
Refreshments: Battlefield Visitor Centre; several good pubs in Market Bosworth.

The Pub

Ye Olde Red Lion Hotel. (GBG)
A welcoming traditional pub and hotel that is over 400 years old. The large bar has an open fire in winter and retains the original oak beams. Food and a good range of cask ales.

For walk C see page 68.

Walks A and B

Facing the Visitor Centre walk to the left of it through a car parking area. Go through a gate and now walk with a hedge on the left through four fields to reach a parking area. (We are here on the Leicester Round, a long distance circular walk centred on Leicester, that we shall follow, with one short break, to Market Bosworth.) Leave this through a gate on the left and turn right along a road. Pass a road on the left to reach, on the left an entrance to the Church of St James, Sutton Cheney. This is well worth a visit.

Church of St James. The oldest part is the nave which is early thirteenth century, although the furnishings are mainly eighteenth century. There are some fine box pews, those in the south-west corner being particularly interesting. A piece of rough wall that supports the south wall of the tower may be part of an earlier building.

There are a number of interesting memorials in the church, the oldest being a stone slab dated 1567 to Margaret Neal in the south wall of the chancel. Opposite is the tomb of Sir William Roberts, who died in 1633 and who built the nearby almshouses; his coat of arms can be seen on the Manor House opposite the church. His much defaced tomb has been moved around the chancel and has separated him from his two wives who now look down from the north wall, presumably keeping an eye on him!

Most prominent is the modern memorial to Richard III whose troops passed the church on their way to battle and who, according to local tradition, heard mass in the church for the last time on 22 August 1485.

Retrace your steps to the road and take the driveway to the left of the entrance path to the church passing Church Cottage on your left and Bumblebee Cottage on your right. Then, after passing the entrance gate to

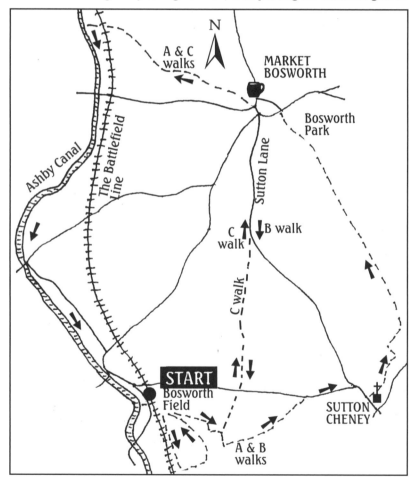

another house continue forward along a grassy path. On reaching tarmac go left through a hedge gap (yellow marker post) and take a path that cuts off diagonally the right-hand corner of the field.

Reaching a hedge corner swing right with a hedge on the right, go through a hedge gap and then go diagonally left across a field (now rejoining the Leicester Round) aiming for another yellow marker post. *This is not strictly the right of way as shown on the OS map which shows the right of way going parallel to the hedge on the right to meet a cross paths where you should turn left to reach the marker post. However, on my last visit the path parallel to the hedge had been cropped whereas the diagonal path had been cleared and was, presumably, the preferred route.* Reaching the post turn right and walk with a hedge on your right. At the end of the field, and by another yellow post, go through a gap and then swing half left to cross a track and follow a path, aiming towards a red roofed house in the trees ahead.

At a hedge corner with a yellow post walk with a hedge on the left passing beneath power lines. Reaching another, now familiar, yellow post continue forward with woodland now on the right passing an old disused sluice gate and crossing a stream. The local authority are to be congratulated on their waymarking, even if it is something of a eyesore!

After a gentle climb pass the red roofed house on your right and now, following another yellow post go forward across grass and through a small patch of woodland. Cross a stile, noticing around here the attractive 'Keep dogs on leads, please' signs designed by Sarah Cumberland, aged 7. Follow the tree-lined path passing Looking Glass Pool on the left, the path becoming lined with lots of giant hogweed. (*Caution! Do not touch this. The fine hairs can cause intense skin inflammation.*). Go through a gate, cross a track and swing slightly left to go forward into woodland, passing a seat on the right.

You are now in Market Bosworth Park that you may wish to explore further.

When, after a few metres, you reach a crossing of tracks go forward towards a yellow marker post (passing two tracks on the right and one on the left), noting that the trees in this small arboretum are labelled with their names. At a cross-paths turn right by a seat to reach Bow Pool (that you may like to walk around): here turn left to join a gravel path. An enclosed path passing houses on the left will enable you to avoid some of the gravel. Ignore a path on the left and reach a road, cross this and go forward past a memorial garden and a No Entry sign into Market Bosworth and Ye Olde Red Lion Hotel on the right. Turn left to reach The Square.

✪ *C walk joins, and public transport users start, here.*

For the shorter Walk B now follow the section 'Market Bosworth to Bosworth Field' on page 69.

From The Square walk north with the bus stop on your left and turn left along Station Road, passing the Dixie Grammar School founded in 1601. Opposite the King William IV pub turn right along Back Lane and when this swings right take a track on the left passing a stile on the right. Continue along the track, passing a school and its playing fields on the left. When the track swings sharp right to a gate go forward to cross a stile and follow a waymarked path with a fence on the left.

Cross a stile and go right, passing to the left of an ivy-clad tree and aiming for a junction of three hedges. Here go through a gate (beside two now redundant stiles) and walk with a hedge and fence on your left. Follow the boundary for about 50 metres and then, when it swings left, continue forward aiming for a hedge corner ahead. Here cross a stile and walk with a hedge on the right to cross a stile, then cross a bridge over the Battlefield Line.

Cross a stile and go forward, then after about 25 metres turn right over another stile and continue your original bearing to reach a bridge over the Ashby Canal. Cross this and turn left onto the towpath, then turn right to walk along this. Now follow the towpath for about 2¾ miles/4.5 km. At the moorings just before bridge 42 note the metal mile post inscribed 15 15, the distances to the original end points of the Ashby Canal. About 100 metres after bridge 41 and beside a seat there is one of the original milestones, now very worn.

The Ashby Canal was originally planned to provide a through route from the River Trent at Burton to the Coventry Canal. However, the section north of Moira which would have provided a link from coalfields near Ashby de la Zouch would have been very

Along the Ashby Canal

expensive to build, requiring locks, reservoirs, pumping engines and possibly a tunnel. When the Ashby coalfields proved less productive than expected the northern section was abandoned but the profitability of the canal was established when a new mine at Moira produced excellent coal that was greatly in demand in London and the south. In the twentieth century subsidence led to the abandonment of the canal north of Snarestone where it now terminates. The Ashby Canal is beautifully rural and the section that we follow has been designated as a conservation area. It is rich in wild life with dragonflies, heron, moorhens and kingfishers.

Approaching Shenton the canal crosses a minor road by a fine brick aqueduct. Reaching bridge 35 go under this and turn right up to the road to cross the canal, then follow the road for about 300 metres to Shenton station and walk through the car park where you will find a Bosworth Battlefield information board.

The Battlefield Line. *Shenton station was originally one of the stations on the Ashby and Nuneaton Joint Railway, opened in 1873, taken over by the LMS railway in 1923, and officially closed in 1970. However, this was not the end of the railway for the five mile section between Shackerstone and Shenstone, now known as the Battlefield Line, is operated by volunteer members of the Shackerstone Railway Society. Trains run between Shenston and Shackerstone Saturdays and Sundays, April to November with some special services at Christmas and some other times. For details: Phone 01827 880754, Talking Timetable 01827 880754, www.Battlefield-Line-Railway.co.uk*

Cross the railway line and turn right along a gravel path.

The Battle of Bosworth Field *took place on 22 August 1485 and dramatically changed the course of English History (and when, in Shakespeare's play, he offered his 'kingdom for a horse'). With the death of Richard III, the last English king to die in battle, it led to the end of the feud between the houses of York and Lancaster, known as the Wars of the Roses and a new king, Henry VII, the first of a Tudor dynasty.*

The battle is traditionally believed to have been fought on Ambion Hill, although some recent research has suggested that it may have been on a different site, to the south west and just across the border into Warwickshire. However, as you walk around you will find many illustrated information boards based on the traditional view.

On reaching Ambion Wood turn left and walk along the edge of the wood, leaving it by a gate. Now follow the stony path, passing King Richards' Well where, according to tradition, the king took a drink from the spring here before the battle. The well is now enclosed by a stone cairn, built in the early part of the nineteenth century. Go through a gate, near to the point where the king was killed, and go forward across grass to the Visitor Centre and the car park.

However, there is still more of the battlefield to be seen so to visit this follow the signpost direction 'Battle Trail and Shenton Station' and follow the waymarks that take you around Ambion Hill to the station, then retrace your steps back to the centre.

If you started from Market Bosworth now continue reading from page 63.

One of the information boards on the Battle Trail

Walk C

Follow the section 'Bosworth Field to Market Bosworth' below, then continue reading from ✪ on page 65.

Bosworth Field to Market Bosworth

From the Visitor Centre walk north up a road with the Centre on your right and a view of Market Bosworth church ahead on the horizon. Follow the road down to a T-junction, cross a footbridge opposite, go through a gate and walk forward across a field, aiming for a hedge gap. *The line of the path tends to vary, not always strictly following the route shown on the OS map. On my last visit I had to turn left beside the hedge for about 100 metres before turning right to reach the corner of the field. However, the path had been kept clear of crops so appeared to be the preferred route.* Go through the gap and swing slightly left from your original bearing to walk north to meet the left-hand edge of a hedge ahead (which, since it looks as though its only function would be as a wind break, may perhaps be removed).

From the end of the hedge veer right to reach a hedge corner, then walk briefly with a hedge on your left to reach and cross a footbridge. Now walk with a hedge on the right, go through a hedge gap and turn right to walk round two sides of a field and go through another hedge gap (marked by a yellow marker post) in the right-hand corner of the field. (*The right of way as shown on the OS map does go directly across but when I was here the field was cropped and the farmer had left a good margin around the edge of the field which was well walked.*) Continue with a hedge on the right until about two thirds of the way along the field cross a footbridge on the right onto the quiet, oak-lined, Sutton Lane and turn left along this.

Leave Sutton Lane through a gate and carry on, then pass an old pump to reach Market Bosworth Square. The Old Black Horse Inn is on the right; turn right along Main Street for the Ye Olde Red Lion.

Market Bosworth to Bosworth Field

From the Square walk south, passing the Old Black Horse Inn on your left, pass Shenton Lane, and then turn right along Sutton Lane, signed Sutton Cheney, Gated Road. Note the old pump on the corner. Soon go through the gate and follow the lane for just over a kilometre/about three quarters of a mile, then immediately past two willows on the right turn right to cross an easily missed, but signposted, footbridge. Turn left and walk down the edge of the field, go through a hedge gap and continue forward with a hedge on the left to another hedge gap about 50 metres to the right of the left-hand corner of the field. (*The right of way as shown on the OS map does go directly across but when I was here the field was cropped and the farmer had left a good margin around the edge of the field which was well walked.*) Go through this and walk straight forward with a hedge on the left, leaving the field to cross a footbridge.

Turn right and walk round the edge of the field for about 40 metres, then, as the boundary swings away to the right go straight ahead to meet the right-hand end of a hedge. Reaching this, and a waymark post, swing left (south) and, moving diagonally away from the hedge on your left, aim towards the far right-hand corner of the field. *The line of the path tends to vary, not always strictly following the route shown on the OS map! On my last visit it took me to a hedge and I had to turn left along this for about 100 metres to reach the corner of the field. However, the path had been kept clear of crops so appeared to be the preferred route.* In the corner go through a hedge gap and walk straight forward aiming towards a road leading up the battlefield. You will probably be able to see the battlefield flag on Ambion Hill. Go through a gate, cross a footbridge and go straight up the road, passing the coats of arms of the Duke of Norfolk and the Earl of Northumberland (the protagonists in the battle) to reach the Visitor Centre and the car park.

10

Birdwatchers Paradise

Coombe Abbey

Special Feature: Capability Brown's landscaped gardens in Coombe Abbey Country Park.

This is just a short walk with no pub en route, though there are three in Brinklow which is about two miles away. I had originally designed a longer walk that went through Brinklow but, apart from the pubs, this was not very interesting with a lot of tarmac. However, Coombe Abbey Park has much to commend it, especially for its wild life (there is a bird hide). A good outing for children.

Distance: 4 km/2½ miles.
Start: Coombe Abbey Country Park (GR403798).
Map: Explorer 221/222; Landranger 140.
Car Parking: Pay and Display car park at Coombe Abbey Country Park (GR403798)
Public Transport: Bus service 585 Coventry/Rugby to Coombe Abbey Country Park car park. Use this service also if you want to go to Brinklow – but note that although some buses go through the village, others just stop by the Bulls Head on the B4027.
Terrain: Easy walking with no hills.
Refreshments: Refreshment facilities in the Country Park; Pubs in Brinklow .

The Pubs
There are three pubs in Brinklow: **The Bulls Head**, **The White Lion** and **The Raven**. All serve cask ales with guest beers. My favourite is the White Lion which has a charming traditional interior.

Coombe Abbey *was founded by Cistercian monks in 1150 but in 1540, following the dissolution of the monasteries, it fell into the hands of Henry VIII. In 1581 it was acquired by John Harrington who built a new house that incorporated parts of the Abbey building, including the cloisters which still exist. In 1603 Princess Elizabeth, daughter of James I, came to live and be educated at Coombe Abbey.*

In the seventeenth century it was acquired by the Craven family and in 1634 William Craven was licenced by Charles I to enclose 650 acres and it is thought that this was the origin of Coombe Abbey Park.

The lake in Coombe Abbey Park

The West Wing (which overlooks the gardens today) was added in 1682, the architect being William Winde, who also designed Buckingham House which later became Buckingham Palace. In 1771 the gardens and surrounding land were re-designed by Lancelot 'Capability' Brown who is considered by many to be England's greatest landscape gardener: in the 1860s the gardens on the south and west side were landscaped by William Andrew Nesfield who also constructed the moat and canal leading to the lake.

In 1923 the Abbey and its grounds were sold to a Coventry builder, John Gray, who, in 1950, leased it to the General Electric Company as a residential training centre. In 1964 the Abbey and its estate were purchased by Coventry City Council and its development into a hotel was begun. The Visitor Centre was opened in 1993 and the fine hotel in 1994.

Walk through the Visitor Centre and at its far end go forward along tarmac, passing a parking area on the right. Cross the walkway over the lake and turn left over a wooden bridge, then swing left to walk with the lake on your left, ignoring paths off. When you reach a gate leading into a conservation area and the heronry (not generally open to the public) turn right – though you may first wish to turn left to the bird hide that looks out across the lake and into the woodland. This contains three fine illustrated panels, one about herons and the heronry, the others illustrating the extensive wildlife in the park.

Follow the path round, now on the edge of woodland. Keep to the main track, ignoring minor paths off. After about 750 metres pass a simple seat on the left and then reach a Y-junction. Here go left, now on the Centenary Way, to reach a grassy area and follow the track across this to reach a Centenary Way waymark at a T-junction. Turn right here, then at another T-junction turn right again. Approaching a third T-junction look on the left for the first of the four tree sculptures that we meet. This shows a sparrow hawk, a woodcock and a badger.

At the T-junction turn left to cross a stream. Over this turn left along a path to walk beside the stream, passing a wooden walkway on the right. At a Y-junction continue forward, still with the stream on your left, the path soon making a U-turn to leave the stream. Pass a pond on the right with a board illustrating the pond's animal life. After two more similar boards another on the left illustrates plant life in the pond.

Reaching a crosstracks and toilets and refreshments go straight forward across a bridge to see, a little further on, and just before reaching a grassy area, another tree sculpture on the right, this one of an owl. Now return to the crosstracks and turn right, passing Top Pool on the left and follow a fence bounding a delightful wild flower meadow. Just to the right look out for a tree carving of a capuchin monk on a grassed mound. When the path forks, go right.

Here you can, if you wish, first go left to briefly leave the park to view the rear of Coombe Abbey with its interesting clock tower. Then return to the fork and turn left.

Pass on the left a dogs' cemetery dating back to the 1880s and reach the formal gardens fronting the abbey, with two stone fish beside the gate into the gardens. Don't take the path immediately beside the gardens but the one to the right of this and look out on the right for the fourth tree carving, this one of a child in a tree. Go back towards the gardens and descend steps, guarded by two griffins. Turn right beside the lake, cross the walkway over the lake and go forward to reach the Visitor Centre and the car park.

One of the tree sculptures in Coombe Park

11

A Saxon Sanctuary

Wootton Wawen

Special Features: Wootton Hall, St Peters Church and the Saxon Sanctuary, Wootton Wawen.

Distance: A: 13 km/8 miles; B: 9.5 km/6 miles.
Start: Wootton Wawen, on the Stratford Road (A3400) (GR154632).
Maps: Explorer 220; Landranger 151.
Parking: Roadside on the B4089 near to its junction with the A3400 (GR153632).
Public Transport: Train: Birmingham/Stratford service to Wootton Wawen (request stop). From the station turn right along the B4089, then on reaching the A3400 turn right to reach the starting point.
Refreshments: The Bull's Head, Wootton Wawen.
Terrain: Easy walking along field paths, lanes and canal towpath, and through some attractive woodland. About half a mile of main roads but good pavements.

The Pub

The Bull's Head, Wootton Wawen
One of the oldest buildings in the county and although having been somewhat modernised recently it still retains its character and many of its period features – oak beams, open fires and stone floors. A Banks' pub with good food and the usual Banks' cask ales.

Wootton is derived from 'Wudutun' meaning (Old English) 'farmstead in or near a wood'; Wawen from Wagen, a Saxon thegn (lord) of Wootton about whom very little is known.

From the B4089 walk along the A3400 Stratford Road past the shops and turn right along a driveway just before reaching a post box and opposite the entrance to Wootton Hall. Cross a grassy area, go through a kissing gate and walk along an embankment with the River Alne over to the left. *The origin of these banks and ditches is unknown. A ford across the Alne here is pre-Roman.* When the path starts to descend cross the River Alne by a footbridge and swing right to go through another kissing gate under power lines. Continue forward to go through two more kissing gates and, keeping a fence on the left, continue until you reach a lane via a gate.

Turn left along the lane, then after about 50 metres and opposite Five Oaks Cottage turn right along a driveway to reach a bridge over the Stratford-upon-Avon Canal. Do not cross this but turn left to walk along the towpath. Cross the Stratford Road by an aqueduct, pass a boatyard and continue along the canal, passing two bridges. You are now on a section of the Monarch's Way. Reaching a third footbridge (No. 51) cross this and walk along a tree-lined bridlepath that can be muddy in places but there are path detours in the worst areas. After about 800 metres/half a mile the path (an ancient track) takes you into Austy Wood.

Austy is a probable mis-spelling of Horstow, meaning a hallowed place, but whether this relates to the early Christians or maybe earlier Druids is not known. The boundary hedges indicate (see page 95) that the wood has been here for over a thousand years

Continue up the gentle incline for about 800 metres/half a mile. Shortly after reaching the top of the slope pass a footpath on the right and go through a wicket gate into a field. Turn right and walk round the edge of the field, soon descending steeply and leaving the field through a hedge gap in its far right-hand corner to reach Cutler's Farm. Pass to the right of farm buildings, now converted into commercial premises, and turn left along a concrete driveway. Soon swing right, then left, to go through a gate and walk north with a stream on your right following a gently ascending farm track. Reaching two gates go round or through the right-hand one into a field and now walk

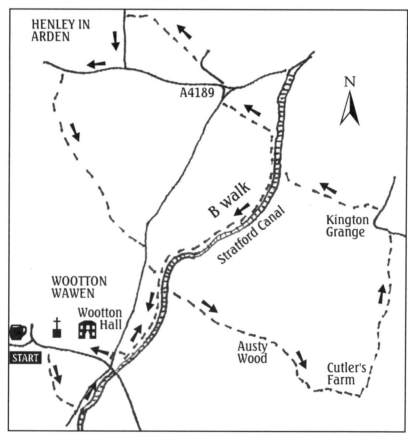

Canal aqueduct at Wootton Wawen

with a fence on the left, leaving it by a gate and following a path between hedge and fence.

Cross a stile beside a gate and walk along an enclosed path to reach the driveway to Chestnut Rise Farm. Turn right to reach a road and go left along this, passing an interesting timber-framed and buttressed farm building. The road swings right passing Kington Farm and about 50 metres past the last of the farm buildings turn left to cross a stile into a field. Walk straight forward and turn left along the field boundary to reach a stile in the corner of the field. *This is to follow the right of way as shown on the OS map although a waymark arrow points directly to the stile.* Cross the stile and very shortly turn right along a broad track.

Across to the right is Barnmoor Wood in which there is an ancient hill fort enclosed by a double bank and ditch, the history of which is unknown. Kington means 'the farm or estate of the king' but which king this refers to is unknown.

Follow the track until a gate takes you into a field and here continue forward towards power lines, passing under these to leave the field by a gate about 25 metres to the left of the field's right-hand corner. Walk diagonally right across the next field to reach the Stratford Canal at bridge 49, just to the left of a wooden fence. Cross the bridge.

Here walks A and B separate. For the shorter walk B now continue reading from ✪ on page 76.

Following the longer walk turn right and walk along the towpath for about 100 metres passing a sluice gate which allows water to be drained from the canal into a stream. Turn left over a stile and across a footbridge to go straight forward across a field, leaving it through a gap to the right of a group of oaks. Now follow a tractor track through a gate to reach a road. Here turn right and then left at a Y-junction. Cross the main road and walk up the lane ahead. When the lane swings sharply right down towards a farm take the rightmost of the two waymarked paths (a driveway) that you can see ahead. Pass a house on the left and enter a field by a stile beside a gate.

Go diagonally left across the field to cross a stile of sorts in a fence, somewhat to the right of the centre of the fence. Cross a green lane, then another stile and walk forward across the field to a stile in the facing hedge about 50 metres to the left of the far right-hand corner. Cross the next field to the far right-hand corner, go over a stile and walk with a hedge on the right to reach a road. Turn left along this and follow it until you reach the A4189 and turn right along this. After about 500 metres, and immediately before reaching Arden Road on the right, cross the road carefully and turn left and take a footpath by the side of Blackford Mill Cottage. Go through a kissing-gate and walk with a hedge on the right. Cross a stile and pass to the left of some barns, then cross a stile a few metres to the left of a gate and continue forward to pass to the left of a house.

Pass a waymark sign and go forward across a field as indicated by the waymark arrow aiming towards a large group of trees at the far end of the field. Reaching the trees walk with them on your right, now being joined by the meandering River Alne that we follow for about two-thirds of a mile. *The path, as I walked it, followed beside the river, although the OS map shows that it should be rather more direct.* Pass under power lines, cross a stile and go diagonally left across a field to reach a road via a stile in the field corner about 50 metres or so to the right of a house. Turn right along the road, very shortly crossing the Alne. About 100 metres after the bridge turn left along a path (having ignored an earlier waymark at a tarmac drive). Follow the tree-lined path which brings you back to bridge 51, crossed on the earlier part of your walk. Turn right along the towpath having now rejoined walk B.

Now continue reading from ☆ below.

❸ Continuing the shorter walk, after crossing the bridge turn left. *The split in the centre of the bridge was designed to allow the towrope to pass through, a common form of bridge construction on the Stratford Canal. This was a cheaper method than the more extensive brick bridges that are commonly met elsewhere on the canals system.*

☆ Follow the towpath back towards Wootton and on reaching bridge 53 turn right along tarmac signed to a Craft Centre and the Saxon Sanctuary. On reaching a road turn left, then at a main road turn right past the Craft Centre, cross the Alne once more noting the 1806 milestone set into the central pillar of the bridge balustrade and carrying the inscription *London 100 miles, Stratford on Avon 6, Henley in Arden 2, Birmingham 18*. Admire the pool and waterfall in the grounds of Wootton Hall that can be seen through the trees.

Reaching the gates of Wootton Hall pass through these and walk along the drive, lined with limes, towards the hall.

Wootton Hall *was built in the seventeenth century in Italian Renaissance style by the second Viscount Carrington, a staunch Catholic who wanted a grand house as a centre for Catholicism in Warwickshire. The coat of arms of the Carrington family can be seen on the front of the building. The hall was used as a hospital in both world wars. The roof was ruined by a fire in 1941 and has been restored. It is in private ownership and is not open to the public. Beside the hall is the uniquely situated village post office, the sunken garden beside it being the remains of the Hall's Italian Gardens.*

Return along the drive and then, just before reaching the road pass through a wicket gate on the right (Sid's Gate) to reach St Peter's Church.

St Peter's Church. *The first church here was built in the eighth century but no trace of it remains. The present building has seen four major stages of building, details of which are well described in a booklet on sale in the church. This booklet provides an invaluable guide for a tour of the church. The oldest part is the tower which dates from the tenth century (or possibly earlier) although the upper part is fifteenth century. The* **Saxon Sanctuary** *is below the tower in the thirteenth century Lady Chapel and contains a superb exhibition that highlights events and features that have shaped the village and its surrounding areas.*

When you have completed your study of the church go back to the road, cross this and turn right to reach the Bull's Head and an opportunity for some well-earned refreshment. Go left along the B4089 for your car or the railway station.

Pool and waterfall at Wootton Hall

12

By Avon's Willowy Banks
Stratford

Special Features: Holy Trinity Church and Skakespeare's Grave, The Greenway Railway Walk, Stratford Butterfly Farm.

Distance: 11 km/7 miles.
Starting point: Stratford-upon-Avon, Bancroft Gardens (GR206549).
Maps: Explorer 205; Landranger 151.
Car Parking: Several car parks in Stratford: the nearest is close to the start of the walk off the A439, Warwick Road; another is near the Butterfly Farm off Swan's Nest Lane.
Public transport: Train or bus to Stratford.
Refreshments: Inn in Clifford Chambers; plenty of refreshment opportunities in Stratford.

The Pub
The Pen and Parchment, Bridgefoot, Stratford. A popular eighteenth century pub with food and some good cask ales.

We start from the Shakespeare Memorial in Bancroft Gardens. In the centre is Shakespeare, surrounded by Lady Macbeth, Prince Hal, Hamlet and Falstaff, representing Philosophy, Tragedy, History, & Comedy. The memorial was completed in 1888, and was moved here in 1933. Walk down the steps from the memorial and go forward towards the canal basin, then turn left to walk beside it to reach the lock. This is the terminus of the Stratford-upon-Avon Canal and the point where it joins the River Avon. The canal was opened to the river here in 1816 and links to the Birmingham & Worcester Canal at Lapworth. Cross the footbridge, noting the plaques describing the restoration of the canal, and walk with the Avon, with its numerous swans, ducks and geese, on your left.

You may, however, like to first go forward to view the Country Artists Fountain, a metal sculpture made for the celebration of the 800th anniversary of the granting of the charter to the town by Richard I in 1196. It was unveiled by the Queen in 1996.

Very shortly pass the Royal Shakespeare Theatre, erected in 1932 to replace the earlier 1876 theatre which had been destroyed by fire in 1926. Walk through the theatre gardens, pass the landing stage for the chain ferry (constructed in 1937 and the last of its type to be made) and the Brass Rubbing Centre and then, after walking through a grassy area and when the path forks, swing away right towards toilets and pass these on your right to reach the road. Turn left here to enter the churchyard of Holy Trinity Church. *The two rows of lime trees represent, on the left, the twelve tribes of Israel and, on the right, the twelve apostles with Judas Iscariot missing, a twelfth tree, set back from the others, represents St Thomas who replaced Judas.*

The Church of the Holy Trinity. *A church on the banks of the Avon in Stratford is first mentioned in a charter of 845. The present limestone building was begun in 1210 and was built in the shape of a cross. Externally the building has changed little from Shakespeare's time: a wooden spire added in 1675 was replaced with the present stone one in 1763.*

There is a small door let into the massive fifteenth century doors on which there is a sanctuary knocker. Fugitives from justice could use this to claim 37 days safety before facing trial.

William Shakespeare was buried here in 1616, the same church where he was baptised in 1564. There is much to see, including Shakespeare's tomb (for which a charge is made), the commemorative altar tomb to Hugh Clopton, builder of the bridge over the Avon seen at the end of this walk, and, in St Peter's Chapel, the American window unveiled in 1896 and a gift from the people of the United States. Walking through the chancel note

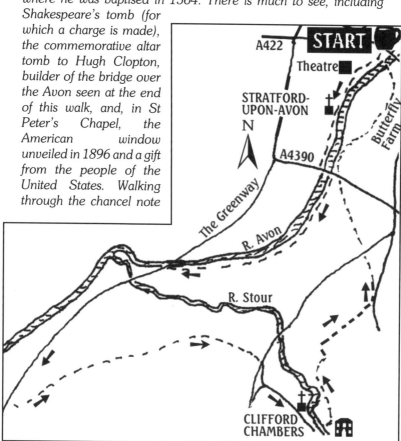

the carved misericords in the choir stalls, both sacred and secular, which illustrate some aspects of fifteenth century life. including angels and mythical beasts and even a man and woman fighting! The oldest part of the building is The Crossing where massive pillars support the tower. Above the vaulted ceiling is the ringing chamber with a magnificent ring of ten bells.

Shakespeare's gravestone bears the words:

Good frend for Jesus sake forebeare,
to digg the dust encloased heare,
Bleste be ye man yt spares thes stones,
And curst be he yt moves my bones.

Holy Trinity Church, Stratford-upon-Avon

Swing right to pass the church and rejoin the road, continuing forward along it. At the end of the road join a paved path, passing the site of Lucy's Mill (now flats), and soon reach a footbridge. Cross the river by this and then turn right, passing under the A4390 to walk beside the river, here on the Avon Valley Footpath. Reaching a modern lock the path swings away from the river and ascends steps into woodland. The lock is one of several that were constructed in the period 1969-1974 and made the Avon once more, after many years of neglect, into a navigable waterway.

Walk through this pleasant woodland with the Avon below on the right, then descend steps and go through two gates before gently ascending into a field. Still with the river as your companion walk through three fields, soon with pollarded willows on the river bank. In the third field pass a steel girder bridge and a brick bridge. Enter another field and after about 25 metres, where a path goes under a bridge, don't follow this but turn sharp right through a gate and go up to reach the Greenway

The Greenway *is a five mile section of what was the old Honeybourne railway line, opened in 1859 and closed in 1976. The route has been developed by Warwickshire County Council since 1989, and is a good surfaced path suitable for cyclists, walkers and wheelchair users.*

Turn left along the Greenway and follow it for about a mile/1.75 km, very soon passing over the River Stour just before its confluence with the Avon.

As you walk you may like to note the variety of trees along the Greenway. I spotted Scots pine, oak, willow, maple, hawthorn, elder, beech, buddleia, dog rose – and others that, with my limited knowledge, I was unable to identify. Apart from the Scots pine these must all have been self-set. I also saw plenty of blackberries and elderberries, and many of the trees were draped with old man's beard.

When you reach a set of concrete traffic barriers, beside a house, and the site of an old railway level crossing and Chambers Crossing Halt, leave the Greenway and turn left along a rough track. However, after swinging left it soon improves. About 100 metres before reaching a farm pass on the left a collapsed wind-pump. After passing the farm the track becomes roughly surfaced, though remaining quiet and peaceful. Follow it for about a mile and a quarter/2 km, about halfway along crossing a lane leading to the sewage works that you might have spotted earlier when walking the Greenway. To the left can be seen Holy Trinity Church.

When the track reaches a road turn right along this and at a Y-junction fork left. Carefully cross the B4632 and pass the New Inn, a seventeenth century coaching inn, now much extended. Now walk into the intriguingly named village of Clifford Chambers. According to the *Oxford Dictionary of English Place Names*, Clifford means a 'ford at a cliff or bank', Chambers refers to the Chamberlain of Gloucester Cathedral who was given the manor in 1099.

Admiring many fine old cottages and larger houses follow this No Through Road to its end just past the Parish Church of St Helen. This will probably be locked but it is worth circling around it to see the fine stonework and gargoyles. On the right of the church is the timber-framed rectory.

According to a village tradition Shakespeare was born in the rectory, his mother having come away from Stratford to avoid the plague. This, doubtless, is not a theory that would find favour in Stratford! However, members of the Shakespeare family did live here and a John Shakespeare gave a bier to the church in 1608.

At its end the road swings left by a timber-framed and thatched house, passing the lovely Manor House on the right.

Manor House. *The original house was destroyed by fire in 1918 and the present building was designed by Sir Edwin Lutyens, one of England's greatest architects. His work ranged from Edwardian country houses to the planning and design of New Delhi in 1912.*

Go through a gate and take a signed path to the left of the entrance to The Old Mill, now a residence. Pass the millpond and the house, swinging round to go up three steps and walk with a fence on the right and the River Stour on the left. Cross the river by a substantial footbridge and then go half left across a small field. Go over a stile, walk straight forward towards the right-hand end of row of trees in the far boundary. Here turn right and walk up to the corner of the field and cross a stile.

Walk between fences, turning right after about 100 metres to pass below a wooden bridge. *Tall people: watch your head!* At a waymarked T-junction of tracks turn left to pass what was originally the Shire Horse Centre (and perhaps due for redevelopment). After passing under power lines turn right to go through a gate, turn right, then immediately left and walk with the power lines and a hedge on your left. The hedge soon ends, but keep the power lines company and then, about 150 metres after going through a hedge gap, turn right to pass a farm (Springfield House) and approach a bridge over a dismantled tramway (*about which more later*) and the A3400. However, don't cross the bridge but turn left along the edge

Clifford Chambers Church

of the field for a few metres to reach a waymark post beside a power post and here turn left to walk diagonally across the field, as waymarked, aiming to its far right corner. Here go over a stile and cross the B4632 to a stile to the right of the driveway to Cross-o'-th'-Hill farm.

Cross this and go diagonally across ridge and furrow to the far corner of the field. Cross a stile to the left of a metal gate, pass farm buildings on the left and a house on the right where you turn right to go along a driveway through a metal gate. Now, keeping a wire fence on the left go straight forward aiming towards the spire of Holy Trinity Church and passing an oak tree after a few metres. Ahead you have a view of a memorial obelisk on the Welcombe Hills. The path swings left and descends, going through a kissing-gate. Continue to descend with the remains of a hedge on the right and on reaching a tarmac path turn right along this. Cross a stile and turn left, still on tarmac, then turn right to briefly join up with the earlier part of the walk and going under the A3400. Pass the footbridge on the left to walk alongside the Avon.

On the other side is the former Lucy's Mill (that we passed earlier) and a weir: beside the path is a information board. *The area to our right is being developed by the local council as a wild life habitat.* Pass another weir and a modern lock and then, just past this cross a footbridge to meet a gravel path as it makes a right-angled bend. Go diagonally forward from this bend, across grass, passing to the left of a small group of trees. Turn right into a car park and go diagonally left across this, aiming towards a children's play area. Turn right to walk along tarmac, passing the children's play area on your left, then go through a kissing gate into the play area, turn right and leave it through another kissing gate and ascend wooden steps to reach the Tramway Walk and turn left along this.

The Tramway Walk. *This follows part of the line of a horse-drawn railway or 'tramway' that once carried goods between the canal and the Avon and Shipston-on-Stour. It was opened in 1826 and extended to Moreton-in-Marsh ten years later. It remained open until the end of the nineteenth century. The Tramway Bridge, soon to be met, is now used as a footbridge.*

Shortly reach the entrance to the Butterfly Farm

The Stratford-upon-Avon Butterfly Farm *contains hundreds of the world's most spectacular and beautiful butterflies in a tropical setting with pools and waterfalls. There are also many fascinating fish, insects and arachnids, including stick insects, beetles, bees, leaf cutting ants, scorpions and the world's largest spider. Open daily except Christmas Day from 10 am to 6 pm (summertime) and dusk (wintertime)*

Cross a road with the Swan's Nest Hotel on the right and go forward to cross the Avon by the Tramway Bridge, looking across to Clopton Bridge on the right Pass Cox's Yard on the right.

In 1839 James Cox established a timber merchant's business here, soon joined by wharves and warehouses along the banks of the River Avon. After the closure of the yard the new Cox's Yard was opened on the site as a tourist attraction with a café, pub, gift shops, theatre and a family games room.

Soon pass one of the original tramway wagons on a length of track. *A memorial commemorates William James, the engineer who considered it to be a natural extension to the Stratford Canal.* On reaching a road cross it to the Tourist Information Centre, to the left of which is the Pen and Parchment and some welcome refreshment at the end of the walk.

13

Medieval Gems

Warwick

Special Features: The historic town of Warwick with its castle and museums; Hatton Country World; the Hatton flight of twenty-one locks.

Distances: A: 18 km/11¼ miles; B: 12.5 km/7¾ miles; (The two walks cross at Hatton Locks so it is possible to switch here if you want to shorten the A walk, or lengthen the B walk). Rail users can shorten either walk by about 2.7 km/1¾ mile by starting at Warwick Parkway station and ending at Warwick.
Start: Warwick Castle town entrance (GR283647), Hatton Locks (GR243669) *or* (rail users): Warwick Parkway station (GR265654)(*the car park here is for rail users only*) .
Maps: Explorer 221; Landranger 151.
Car Parking: In Warwick: The most convenient car park is a Pay and Display in Castle Lane adjacent to Warwick Castle (GR283647). However, this is quite small so if it is full there are other car parks in Westgate, Barrack Street, West Rock, The Butts, Priory Road, Linen Street and St Nicholas Park.
At Hatton: Pay and Display car park at Hatton Locks (GR243669).
Public Transport: Rail or bus to Warwick or rail to Warwick Parkway.
Warwick Route: Leave Warwick station from the platform 2 side and turn left, now following the Centenary Way to reach a grassed area. Turn left under the railway and continue along the tarmac path to reach a road. Go forward along this (Cape Road), crossing to the right-hand side to reach the main road and noting on the side of the house on the corner (Northgate House) a sundial dated 1698. Cross the main road carefully and go forward along Northgate Street towards St Mary's Church. Go under the tower and along Church Street to reach High Street and the fine courthouse. Cross High Street/Jury Street carefully using the pedestrian crossing to the right and then go forward along Castle Street passing the Tourist Office on the corner. Pass the Warwick Doll Museum and the residence of Warwick benefactor Thomas Oakland. This will bring you to a car park and the town entrance to Warwick Castle.
To return to the station turn left along Castle Street, passing some attractive timber-framed buildings. Reaching High Street/Jury Street cross this at the crossing, noting another sundial on the front of Northgate House, and go forward to reach St Mary's Church. Go under the tower and forward along Northgate Street. Reaching a roundabout go right, then immediately left to cross the road and walk

along Cape Road. When this swings left go forward along a tarmac path. Go under the railway bridge and turn right to reach the station.

Warwick Parkway route: Leave the station and turn left to walk through the car park. Leaving it, walk up to traffic lights, turn right across tarmac and take a waymarked footpath beside another set of traffic lights. Cross a stile and now read from ◆on page 88.

Refreshments: The Waterman at Hatton and numerous refreshment opportunities in Warwick.

Terrain: Very easy walking through pleasant Warwickshire countryside with a section along the Grand Union Canal. Some minor ascents but nothing really strenuous. Some tarmac but most of this along quiet minor roads, lanes and drives.

❗ The walks use public rights of way across Warwick Racecourse but these are closed on race days. For information about these dates phone 01926 491553 or visit www.warwickracecourse.co.uk.

The Pubs

The Waterman, Hatton
A handy pub for boatmen, especially towards the end of the slog up the twenty-one locks. Now popular with diners. Three cask ales.

The Old Fourpenny Shop Hotel, Crompton Street, Warwick **(GBG)**
A Grade II listed building dating from around 1800. When the navvies were building the canals this was one of their favourite pubs where they could buy a tot of rum and a coffee for 4d. Good food and six cask ales.

If starting from Hatton Locks go to ✪ on page 90.

Warwick. The town was founded on the banks of the River Avon in AD914 as a defence against Danish invaders. It controlled the river valley, the river crossing on the road to London and the roads to Stratford, Coventry and the salt way to Droitwich.

It contains many buildings of historic interest including one of the country's most dramatic and complete medieval castles that has been inhabited continuously since the Middle Ages.

Many of the central streets were destroyed by fire in 1694 but many buildings were re-built in the handsome style of the late seventeenth and early eighteenth centuries, so contributing to the charm of the town. Several important medieval buildings survived the fire, notably the Lord Leycester Hospital (shortly to be passed), as well as a group of timber–framed buildings that will have been seen by public transport users making their way to the castle.

From the Castle entrance gates walk along Castle Lane with the castle walls on your left and passing Back Lane. About 40 metres before Castle Lane bends right turn right along Leycester Place (beside Kings Lodge). At the T-junction cross the main road carefully to the Lord

Leycester Hospital, a beautiful complex containing a fine half-timbered courtyard, Guildhall, Banqueting Hall, St James' Chapel and a military museum. On the pavement is a fine Victorian pillar-box, cast in 1856 and one of two still in use in Warwick.

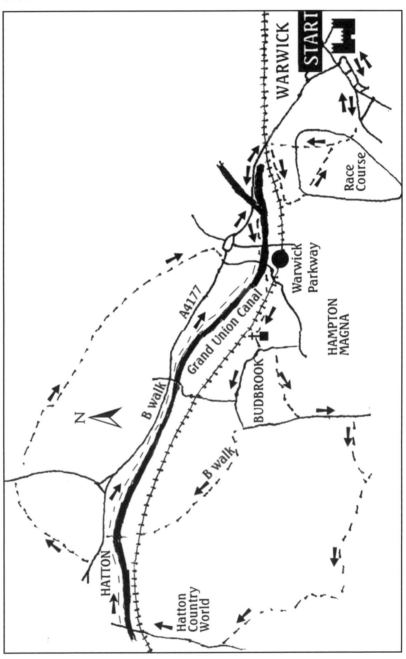

The Lord Leycester Hospital

Lord Leycester Hospital. *The group of buildings that comprise the hospital are dominated by the ancient Chantry Chapel of St James, built over the West Gate into Warwick by the 12th Earl of Warwick in the fourteenth century. The benefice of the Chapel was granted to the Guild of St George on its formation under a license issued by Richard II in 1383. Sometime between 1386 and 1413 the Guild of the Blessed Virgin, based at the Collegiate Church of St Mary, joined the Guild becoming known as the United Guilds of Warwick.*

In 1546, the United Guilds were dispersed by King Henry VIII, but their property was saved from seizure through the foresight of their Master who had it transferred to the Burgesses of Warwick.

In 1571, Robert Dudley, Earl of Leycester acquired the buildings and founded, under charter from Queen Elizabeth I, a Hospital for aged or disabled soldiers and their wives.

For nearly 400 years the administration of the Hospital remained almost unchanged until 1956 when an Act of Parliament replaced it by a Board of Governors, who decided to restore the building and modernise the quarters. Queen Elizabeth, the Queen Mother, opened the Hospital after its restoration, on 3rd November, 1966, and it now houses eight ex-servicemen and their wives in modernised flats.

Turn left, go under the archway, cross Bowling Green Street and continue forward down West Street. On reaching the Wheatsheaf Hotel note the row of timber-framed buildings on the opposite side of the road and then turn right along Crompton Street, cross the A4189 carefully and go into Warwick Racecourse.

Cross the racetrack and go forward to a waymark post and from here go half right to walk about 50 metres to the right of a group of trees and join a golf course. Reach a waymark post and then go forward with a teeing off area on your left and the golf-house and a practice area on your right, walking due north (and watching out for flying golf balls!). Cross the racetrack again and go along a footpath with houses on the right. Pass a footpath on the left, bear right and go forward through a kissing-gate to reach a road, along which turn left under a railway bridge. Across the hedge on the left is the Saltisford Arm of the Grand Union Canal.

Reaching the Dun Cow a stile on the left leads into a grassy picnic area beside the Saltisford Arm and you may wish to walk along this for about 100 metres rather than staying on the road. Leave it as you reach some huts.

Continuing along the road stay on the pavement when it separates from the road and reach a canal bridge. Cross this and the road *carefully*, take steps on the right down to the canal and turn right under the bridge. *There is a well-used path, though not a right of way, on the left that avoids this nasty crossing.* Walk along the towpath with the canal on your left, go under the A46, pass Hatton Bottom Lock and under another road bridge, then turn right to take a footpath up the road and turn right along this. Cross the bridge and. follow the road to reach traffic lights and here take a waymarked path on the right, cross a stile and walk beside the extension car park for Warwick Parkway station.

◆Turn right across a stream to walk beside another parking area, cross a stile, turn left to cross a second stile and walk with a fence on the right towards the railway embankment. Cross a third stile on the right to join a footpath and walk along the edge of a field, the railway line on the left.

At the end of the field go left under the railway and turn half right to walk towards the right-hand side of a group of trees, behind which Budbrooke Church can be seen.

Beside the trees are the remains of a moat that originally surrounded Budebroc Manor, which probably had its origins in the eleventh century. However, the wood and stone building fell into decay in the seventeenth century and was demolished.

Cross a stile and go slightly left across ridge and furrow (*signs of medieval farming*) to leave the field and walk through the churchyard of St Michael's Church, passing the graves of some members of the Royal Warwickshire Regiment who died in World War II. As you leave the churchyard you will pass a weathervane topped with the badge of the regiment (which was amalgamated with other regiments in 1963). It was once a focal point in the nearby Budbrooke Barracks and was presented to the church in 1966

Medieval Gems

St Michael's Church *dates from the twelfth century (when it served the local village of Budebroc. In 1542 the village was wiped out by the Black Death. None of the original village remains and there are now just a few properties located close to the church. The oldest part of the church is the Norman arch, located in the north wall of the nave, which would have provided the main entrance from the medieval village – the low headroom beneath the arch, probably indicates the expected height of the villagers! Largely on account of this arch the church is a Grade I listed building. The present entrance is through a pair of nail studded oak doors, erected in 1668. The tower was probably built in the thirteenth century.*

Walk forward to reach a lane and here the B walk separates from the A walk. For the B walk now continue reading from ✳ on page 93.

Continuing the A walk, turn left along the lane and after about 60 metres turn right along a driveway. Just before the driveway swings right cross a stile on the left and walk half left across a field, leaving it by a stile in the far left corner. *This field is the site of the old village of Budbrooke.* Go through a rough area, then left through a gate and turn right along the right-hand edge of a field to join a lane. Turn left along this as it rises slightly, Hampton-on-the-Hill coming into view ahead. At a T-junction turn right through a kissing-gate and follow a track for about 600 metres, then at a field boundary turn left along a path for about 50 metres to reach a tarmac driveway along which you turn right.

The lane becomes attractively tree-lined as it approaches Grove Park House. Pass Whitehill Wood and at a Y-junction fork left, soon leaving the woodland to continue past a farm. Then, reaching Wilderness Cottage on the right turn right through a gate beside a cattle grid and continue forward along a stony track. Go beside another cattle grid and stay on the track as it swings right and then left. Cross another cattle grid, then leave the track and swing half right to take a path which goes diagonally across a field and roughly parallel with power lines. After going through a hedge gap walk with the field boundary on the left, then after another hedge gap pass through an orchard. At the end of this swing left to reach a road via a stile beside a gate. Turn right along the road and after about 300 metres reach the entrance to Hatton Country World.

Hatton Country World *includes Hatton Shopping Village and Hatton Farm Village. The Shopping Village contains twenty-five shops in quaint streets of converted Victorian farm buildings, with arts and crafts, speciality gift shops, antique dealers, a farm shop with fresh food from local farms and a butchery unit for locally-reared, traditional cuts of meat and homemade sausages. The Farm Village will be of particular interest if you have children with you.*
Open daily 10am-5pm; 27 December-3 January 11am - 4pm, closed Christmas Day and Boxing Day, open until 4pm on Christmas Eve. For details phone 01926 843411.

Leaving Country World continue along the road for about 400 metres and after crossing the railway reach the Grand Union Canal.

The Grand Union Canal originally comprised a number of separate canals (five between Birmingham and London) but the companies were integrated as the Grand Union Canal Company in 1929. A programme of modernisation aided by government funding was launched in 1932, the locks being widened to replace the original narrow locks so that the more efficient broad beam boats could replace the traditional narrow boats. Unfortunately the work was not completed and the canal lost out in the competition from road and rail transport.

Just before reaching the bridge over the canal turn left to descend to the towpath, then turn right along this passing under the bridge, soon to reach the first of the Hatton Locks.

*The magnificent **Hatton flight** consists of twenty-one locks, taking the canal down 150 ft. Passage through these was a daunting task for boatmen – although the pub near to the top lock will have brought some relief. The remains of the old narrow locks can be seen by the sides of the newer widened locks. Straight ahead, though possibly obstructed by trees in the summer, can be seen the tower of St Mary's Church in Warwick.*

When you reach bridge 54 the towpath changes sides so cross here.

⭐ Hatton Locks.

The A and B walks again separate here. For the longer A walk continue from ⮞ *below.*

Walk B now follows the Grand Union Canal (*see above*) for about 3½ km/2 miles but you may first like to visit The Waterman for refreshment. In this case follow the instructions for the first part of the A walk below. As you set off you can see, straight ahead, the tower of Warwick Church. Continuing, walk through pleasant Warwickshire countryside past more locks and steadily descending. Just past lock 27 reach a road bridge. Now continue reading from ● on page 92.

⮞ Continuing the A walk turn left across a car parking area to pass a dry dock on your left, go through a kissing gate and along a path that leads you up to the road and The Waterman pub.

Cross the road *very carefully (there is a dangerous bend)* and turn left along the pavement, then take the first turning right along a waymarked drive towards Home Farm. Pass the farm and a brick building on your left, and go forward through a kissing gate beside a metal gate and follow a tree-lined path as it swings left. Go through another kissing-gate onto a farm track and turn right along this. Walk with woodland on the right and at a Y-junction go right. The woodland is nicely carpeted with bluebells in the spring. Reaching a road turn right for about 50 metres, then turn left along a track for about 350 metres to reach Turkey Farm.

Here go through a gate to pass the farm on your right, then after passing a pool on your left and an oak tree on your right the track bends right. *Warwick church repeatedly comes into view along this next section of the walk.* Follow the track, with a field boundary on your right, almost immediately passing a tree lined pool over to your left. After about 200 metres and reaching a waymark post turn left to walk around the right-hand boundary of a field with a hedge and ditch on the right. Go through a hedge gap and turn right still with the hedge and ditch on the right. Go through a further two fields, passing woodland on the right. The path swings right around the end of the woodland and then joins a track along which you turn left. This meanders around towards Wedgnock Park Farm, then, eventually turns right through a gate along concrete, then tarmac, passing the farm on your left.

With a sound of traffic ahead the tarmac bears right to meet the A4177. Cross the dual carriageway by the pedestrian crossing and go slightly right to go forward along Old Budbrooke Road.

Just past the County Highways Head Office cross the road carefully as though to enter the driveway of Coach House Cottage but then go left to descend along a path down to the canal. Turn left along the towpath to meet a bridge.

Here walks A and B rejoin, and we retrace our steps back to Warwick Castle.

Warwick Castle

● Go under the bridge and past Hatton Bottom Lock, soon passing under the A46(T). After about 350 metres the canal swings left, passing the Saltisford Arm. Very shortly go under bridge 51 and turn left to go up steps to the road.

Just before reaching bridge 51 there is a well-used path on the left, leading up to the road, that avoids the necessity of subsequently crossing it. However, it is not a right of way.

Cross the bridge and walk along the A425, passing Budbrooke Road on the right and, if you took the official route up the steps, very carefully crossing to the other side of the busy road. Stay on the pavement as the road divides at a traffic island and soon pass the Saltisford Canal Centre and the Dun Cow and go under the railway. After a few metres turn right beside housing to go through a kissing-gate and turn right to walk with a fence and the railway line on the right. Reaching a footbridge over the railway turn left into woodland and descend to reach the racecourse.

Swing slightly left, passing a hut on the left, go through the race course barriers to meet a waymark post. This will direct you to cross a ditch to the right of a line of tall trees from where you pass three conifers and cross a footbridge. Continue your bearing (SSE) to walk across the golf course (*watching out for flying balls*) and meet another waymark post. You soon pass to the left of a group of trees on high ground that (if you started from Warwick) you passed on the outward journey. Keep about 50 metres to the left of the trees and meet another waymark post where you swing right, with the golf-house on your left, to reach the entrance to the racecourse. Cross Hampton Street and walk up Crompton Street to very soon reach the Fourpenny Shop Inn.

Continue up to the main road, turn left and cross the road to walk up Leycester Place, then turn left to reach the town entrance to Warwick Castle.

Warwick Castle. *The entrance is by a passage cut through the rock and guarded by two portcullises. Many of the rooms in the castle are open to the public and have been maintained in their original condition. The castle was home to the Dukes of Warwick and was sold to the Tussaud Group in 1978.*

The first castle was built at Warwick in 1086 as part of William the Conqueror's attempt to subdue resistance in the Midlands and Northern England. It was a wooden building on a raised mound, surrounded by a wooden stockade.

The earliest stone building was constructed in the twelfth century though none of this survives today. The East Front, comprising the Gatehouse and two towers known as Caesar's Tower and Guy's Tower, was constructed in the fourteenth century by the 12th Earl of Warwick. Further building was carried out on the north side of the castle by Richard III (1483-5) and the two small towers are parts of this work. The main building of the apartment block dates from the beginning of the seventeenth century.

In 1749 the grounds surrounding the Castle were landscaped by Capability Brown giving broad lawns and magnificent trees. The original castle mound was planted with shrubbery. The beautiful gardens are today backed by a conservatory containing large tropical plants.

Opening Times. Warwick Castle is open all year except Christmas Day. Summer: 10am - 6pm; Winter (October - March): 10am - 5pm. Last admission is half an hour before closing. For more details and admission charges: 0870 4422000.

✳ Walk B: Turn right along the lane. Follow it as it meanders around passing housing and Grange Farm and at a T-junction turn left, signed Hampton-on-the-Hill. When the road makes a right-angled bend left turn right along a track signed Budbrooke Farm. Follow this as it swings left, then right to pass the farm on your left. Where the track turns into the farm turn right through a gate, then immediately left through another gate and go forward with a fence, then a hedge on the left. Cross a stile beside a gate and here go slightly right (NW) to descend along a path to reach a waymark post that will direct you across a footbridge and forward through the following field. Go through a hedge gap and forward, swinging slightly right to meet and cross the railway by a green footbridge. *Over to the right a striking building can be seen; this is a former sanatorium, now converted to housing.*

Follow a footpath, now part of a local nature trail, that takes you through Brook Marsh. *This area was dug out during the building of the railway in 1848 and has remained uncultivated ever since.* Go forward to cross a stile and go up to the Grand Union Canal. Cross the canal by the bridge, giving a good view on both sides of the Hatton Locks.

Now continue reading from ✪ on page 90.

14

A Medieval Map of the World

Hereford

Special Features: Hereford Cathedral and the Mappa Mundi, Hereford Cider Museum, Broomey Hill model railway, The Victory pub and Spinning Dog brewery.

Distance: A: 14 km/8¾ miles;B: 11.25 km/7 miles.
Start: : Hereford Cathedral.
Maps: Explorer 189; Landranger 149.
Car Parking: There are several car parks in Hereford but probably the most convenient is the NCB car park in Little Berrington Street. From the car park turn left, then left again along Berrington Street. Turn right along St Nicholas St and join the walk at 🚗 below.
Public Transport: Buses and rail to Hereford. To join the walk see the box on page 103.
Refreshments: The Victory pub and other pubs and restaurants in Hereford.
Terrain: Some gentle ascents but nothing very strenuous. Pleasant Herefordshire countryside with good views. Final section beside the River Wye. Some tarmac on the first section but after leaving the city this is along quiet country lanes.

The Pub

The Victory and Spinning Dog Brewery, St Owen Street, Hereford. **(GBG) (CM)**
The Victory refers to Nelson's flagship and the bar resembles the interior of an eighteenth century man o' war, all done out in traditional materials with wood, rope and glass. The Spinning Dog honours the pub dog, Cassie, who has a predilection for chasing her tail. Some excellent brews from this microbrewery (you might be able to have a visit) and other good local cask ales and ciders. Good food.

With your back to the west front of the cathedral walk forward along King Street, passing the Tourist Information Centre. Cross Bridge Street into St. Nicholas Street (🚗), cross Victoria Street using the underpass on the left-hand side and continue forward along Barton Road. Cross the bridge over a former railway. Pass Broomy Hill and stay on the main road. Past Rylands Street the main road swings right, but here continue forward along Breinton Road (now, thankfully, peaceful and quiet!), soon passing Hereford Cemetery on the right and the Broomy Hill

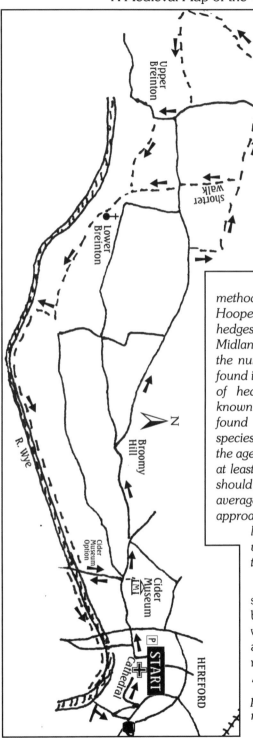

Waterworks with its prominent Italianate water tower on the left and reaching more open country.

At a Y-junction go right, signed Upper Breinton 1¾. Now gently climbing you may be interested to note the variety of tree species in the hedges, generally an indication of their considerable age.

'Hooper's Law'. *Naturalists use a method devised by Dr. Max Hooper in the 1950s for dating hedges in the English Midlands. This is based upon the number of woody species found in a 30m (100 ft.) length of hedge. Using hedges of known age from old maps, he found that the number of species × 100 roughly equals the age of the hedge. However at least three random samples should be taken and an average calculated. As you approach the highest point look back for good views of Hereford and the Malverns.*

Just after passing several buildings and a post box look, at the end of a wall, for an interesting stone at the side of the road that reads:

'This road divided at this point for the convenience of repair 1868'.

Pass a lane and the Halfway House on the left and soon reach the entrance to Little Breinton Farm where there is an old cider press. About 50 metres past the farm turn right along the waymarked bridleway leading to Upper Hill Farm. Follow this as it swings left past a waymark post and then passes Poole Hill farm and a pond, Drovers Pond, which as a board explains, was restored in 1998 in memory of Jamie Bott of Upper Hill. Doubtless we are now following an old drove road. Past Upper Hill Cottage the surfacing disappears and the track becomes a footpath entering a tree lined section. Ignore a stiled path off to the right and emerging from the wooded area reach a crossing path.

Here walks A and B separate. If you wish to follow the longer route A now continue reading from ✪ below.

Taking the shorter route B turn left over a stile and with a fence and orchard on the right walk through three fields. Cross a lane, go over another stile and walk with a hedge on the left. Go through a gap into a second field, soon passing on the left a gate leading into an orchard. Leave the field through a kissing gate to rejoin the longer walk at ★ on page 97.

✪ Taking the longer route continue forward passing under power lines and along a hedge-lined path, then going through a traffic barrier to reach tarmac. After passing housing and reaching a T-junction cross a stile ahead and now walk with a hedge on the right. At the end of the field turn left, still keeping the hedge on the right. At the next corner turn right into woodland (carpeted with bluebells in the spring), cross a stile, immediately swing right, then leave woodland by another stile and turn left to walk through an orchard with a fence and hedge on your left.

Following waymarks keep to the edge of the orchard as it swings right, go up a slight incline and turn left to reach and cross a stile. Continue forward with a fence on your left and a good view of the Black Mountains ahead. At a fence cross a stile – don't be distracted by another stile over to the right – and continue with the fence on your left. Cross a stile and walk along the edge of woodland with a steep drop on your right, very shortly going up three steps on the left to cross a stile, them immediately another stile on the left to walk with a hedge on the right. We are now on the Wye Valley Walk.

Swing right to leave the field through a gate, go forward a few metres passing an old bathtub to reach a gate on your right. Here turn 90° left and resume your original bearing (east). Leave the field through a gate and descend along a track initially enclosed between hedges. The track swings left, then right to reach a road. Turn right here, passing a timber-framed building, and at a T-junction turn right again, signed Breinton Common. Just before the road swings sharp right take a waymarked path on the left, climbing steps to cross a stile. Turn right to walk around the edge of a field with a fence and woodland on the right. Cross a stile and continue beside woodland, then on passing the attractive garden of Breinton Court leave the field through a rather decrepit kissing-gate and turn right.

★ *Here the shorter walk joins the longer walk.* Cross a driveway to go through a gate and half left across an orchard, pass a tennis court and go through a kissing-gate to reach a lane. Cross this, go over a stile and walk half-right through another orchard, leaving it by a stile (waymarked Circular Walk) to the left of a car parking area. Swing left to reach the lichgate to St Michael's Church, Breinton.

The churchyard contains the grave of Canon Gorton who was friend of Sir Edward Elgar and who helped the composer with the text of his oratorio 'The Apostles'. The grave (25 metres ahead from the church porch and identified by a Celtic cross on the headstone) carries a motif (now rather weathered) from the oratorio.

Leaving by the lichgate turn left to walk initially beside the churchyard (surrounded by a ha-ha), then swing left to go through a kissing-gate and follow an enclosed path along the edge of woodland with yet another orchard on the left. Cross a stile and continue beside the woodland, then reaching a metal kissing-gate on the right go through it and walk with a hedge on your left. Almost reaching a wooden fence turn right and descend to a large horse-chestnut tree, then swing left to go through a hedge gap and cross a field to reach a stile. Cross this and turn left along the River Wye, now rejoining the Wye Valley Walk.

Approaching Hereford you can see the Italianate waterworks tower that was passed on the way out and soon Hereford Cathedral ahead. On your left you will pass the Broomy Hill miniature railway – an attraction if you have children with you.

The Broomy Hill Miniature Railway *is operated by the Hereford Society of Model Engineers. At is open on the last Sunday of each month, April-October, 12-5pm. Admission is free with a small charge for rides on the trains, usually with steam locomotives.*

When you reach Hunderton Bridge, carrying a disused railway, now converted into a cycleway/walkway, go up steps onto this. This bridge was built for the Newport, Abergavenny and Hereford Railway and opened in 1854.

You now have another choice of routes, either to follow the main route to the Cider Museum or return directly to the starting point. For the shorter alternative now continue reading from ✳ *on page 98.*

Turn left along the cycleway/walkway, then when you reach a bridge don't go under it but turn left and then right up to the main road. Go left along this for about 50 metres and then take the tarmac pathway on the right beside house no. 6. Reaching a roadway continue forward and follow the road to a T-junction. Here turn right and after a few metres pass the main entrance to the King Offa Distillery. Just past this turn right along a path to reach the Cider Museum and the Distillery.

Hereford Cider Museum

The Hereford Cider Museum *tells the story of traditional cider-making and shows how apples were gathered, milled, pressed and the juice fermented to make cider. The museum contains a reconstructed farm ciderhouse with all the traditional cider makers' materials. A coopers' workshop displays the tools used for making barrels over four centuries. Opportunities to sample and purchase ciders, cider brandy and liqueurs. Open daily April-October 10 am-5.30 pm; Nov-March Tues-Sun 11 am-3.00 pm. Phone 01432 354207.*

Now retrace your steps back to the river.

✳ Cross the bridge and descend to carry on along the right bank of the river. Pass under an incredibly ugly modern bridge to reach the delightful Wye Bridge built in 1490, damaged in the Civil War, and widened in 1826.

Hereford and the Civil War. *Although Charles I had considerable support in Herefordshire, Hereford was occupied by parliamentary forces in September 1642. However, the occupation proved difficult to maintain and in December the troops left and the city reverted to the royalists. Nevertheless, its defences were inadequate and in April 1643 a parliamentary force marched north from Gloucester and easily re-occupied Hereford. But their commander still lacked sufficient strength to maintain his position and was forced to withdraw from the county, marching out of Hereford on 20 May.*

Although the royalists began to reorganise local defences their position was not secure. On 18 June 1645 Charles arrived in Hereford but his attempts to raise more troops in the county failed. Meanwhile a Scottish army in the service of Parliament was moving south and laid siege to Hereford on 31st July.

The city held out for five weeks, two of the city's churches and an arch of the Wye Bridge being destroyed. On 1 September news reached the besiegers that the king was approaching with a relieving force. The Scottish army withdrew and Charles entered the city on 4 September.

Colonel Scudamore, the city commander was knighted and the siege was commemorated by the addition to the city coat of arms of ten saltires (white crosses) representing the ten divisions of the Scottish army encircling the city. The motto, 'Invictae fedelitatis praemium', translates as 'The reward of Invincible Loyalty'.

However in December that year Hereford again fell to the Parliamentarians by means of a clever trick. Six soldiers were disguised as workmen employed to break the ice on the city moat. The sentries who came to check their identities were quickly overpowered and Parliamentary troops who were hiding nearby rushed in and after a short struggle the city fell.

You now have another choice – to return directly to the Cathedral or to first visit the site of Hereford Castle and/or take refreshment at the Victory pub.

For the Cathedral cross the bridge and opposite the Black Lion turn right along a passageway, soon passing on the right a plaque on the wall recording the site of the birthplace of Nell Gwynne in 1650, the house having been demolished in 1858. Reaching the Cathedral (see page 101), and the end of the walk, pass on the right the gatehouse of the Bishop's Palace.

For the Castle and the pub cross the road and carry on beside the river. As you pass the Saracen's Head note its fine cast iron balcony. If you look back to the Wye Bridge you will see a black pipe on its side. This is the remains of a Victorian urinal that was originally on the bridge! Soon pass a memorial (and a warning) to those who have drowned in the River Wye. We are here walking through the Bishops Meadow which was given to the city by the Cathedral, the leasehold in 1914 and the freehold in 1937. It was opened by Queen Mary in 1937. Note several interesting tree sculptures, one of which on the left is of a bulldog. Here a plaque records an incident in 1898 when a bulldog named Dan, owned by Dr George Robertson Sinclair, the Cathedral organist, fell into the river nearby during a walk with Sir Edward Elgar. This incident is allegedly recorded in variation number 11 (GRS) of Elgar's *Enigma Variations*. Elgar lived in Hereford between 1904 and 1911 and wrote many of his major works here.

Reach the fine Victoria Bridge, constructed in 1897 to commemorate Queen Victoria's Diamond Jubilee and replacing an earlier ferry. Note the Hereford coat of arms on each of the stone pillars. Cross this when you now have another alternative: to return to the cathedral via Castle Green, the site of Hereford Castle, or via the Victory pub and Spinning Dog brewery. For the pub route continue reading from ✳ on page 102.

For Castle Green, turn left up steps and at the top turn right to walk on tarmac around the embankment, noting the fine Victorian gas lamps, now converted. Below on the left is a bowling green and on the side of the hut is an information board describing the area and its history. When you turn left you ascend slightly: this is Hogg's Mount and is thought to be the site of a motte and bailey where the first castle was situated.

The Green encloses the area which contained Hereford Castle and if you are walking in a very dry period the outline of the castle's buried walls may be apparent in lines of parched grass. Soon pass on the right the remains of the moat.

Hereford Castle. *The first castle predated the Norman Conquest and was built about 1046, probably of timber. In 1055 the castle was overrun by the Welsh, the town and the cathedral were burnt, and the castle was destroyed.*

In 1066 William fitzOsbern, Earl of Hereford, was charged with building castles along the Welsh border. He restored the castle which became the focus of the city's defences and a royal stronghold until the Civil War, after which it went into decline and was eventually demolished, largely in the 1650s, the area – Castle Green – becoming a public open space. Little of its history is visible today, other than the surrounding earthworks and part of the moat.

In the centre of the green is Nelson's Column, not so tall as that in Trafalgar Square but erected in 1809 for the same purpose; to honour a national hero. On the side is a relief of Nelson (a statue on top proved too expensive!) with below a commendatory inscription claiming that his successes had demonstrated to the French and the Spanish 'the naval superiority of Great Britain'. Nelson visited Hereford several times and in 1802 he was granted the freedom of the city.

Follow round the Green until you reach a stone building overlooking the river. This is Castle Cliff, the only remaining part of the castle. It has been a prison, the Castle Governor's lodge, and is now a Hereford Community Service Training centre. Here turn right along tarmac passing a green on the right and meeting Castle Hill joining from the right. Here look across to the right of a house named St Ethelberts for St Ethelbert's Well.

St Ethelbert's Well *was once famed for the reputed healing properties of its waters. Ethelbert was King of East Anglia but was murdered by Offa, King of Mercia in the eighth century. Attempts to dispose of Ethelbert's body proved difficult with miraculous lights appearing over the grave wherever it was buried. Eventually his body was taken to Hereford for re-burial, and where it was rested momentarily a spring gushed up that became known as St. Ethelbert's Well.*

Hereford Cathedral and the River Wye

Continue forward along Quay Street where you pass, on your right, a half-timbered barn and a rare Edward VII letter box, painted black and no longer in use. Reaching Castle Street turn left, go through a gate and then fork left to visit Chapter House Yard and College Cloisters and enter the Cathedral by the St John's Door entrance.

Hereford Cathedral. There has been a cathedral on this site beside the River Wye since Saxon times, built over the tomb of King Ethelbert who, after his canonisation became the patron saint of the cathedral. There was a major rebuilding after the Norman Conquest and much of this work can be seen inside the cathedral. Over the centuries there have been many additions with the central tower being added in the fourteenth century and the cloisters in the 1470s.

Much wilful damage was done at the time of the Reformation with more damage during the Civil War and in 1786 the entire west end collapsed. This was reconstructed but further changes were made in the 1900s. Consequently the cathedral provides a wonderful display of a range of architectural styles and fashions.

In the fifteenth century south-west cloister is the New Library Building which houses two of Britain's most important historical treasures – the medieval Mappa Mundi and the Chained Library, together with models, artifacts and computer technology that tell the stories of these jewels. The Chained Library contains over 1,500 rare books dating from the eighth to the nineteenth centuries.

*The **Mappa Mundi** is a remarkable medieval treasure, drawn on a piece of vellum, which illustrates how thirteenth century scholars* *viewed the world, geographically and spiritually. It is undated but evidence indicates that it was made by Richard de Bello in the diocese of Lincoln around 1290. It provides a fascinating insight into the then current views of man's history and the marvels of the natural world and its inhabitants.*

Opening hours: Easter to October 10 am-4.15 pm (Suns 11 am-3.15 pm); November to Easter 11 am-3.15 pm (Suns closed). Phone 01432 374202.

✳ For the Victory go up to the road and turn left along Mill Street, pass Cantilupe Street on the left and continue along Mill Street past traffic No Entry signs. Pass Green Street and go forward along a passageway, then turn right to reach the Victory.

After refreshment turn left after leaving the pub, continue forward at the crossroads and reaching St Ethelbert's Street turn left along this. At the end turn right along Castle Street to reach the Cathedral, passing St Ethelbert's Hospital, built of red sandstone in 1805, with a fine plaque above the door. Approaching the Cathedral go through a gate and fork left to visit Chapter House Yard and College Cloisters, then enter the Cathedral by the St John's Door entrance.

The bar of The Victory

Public transport

Rail: To reach the starting point from the railway station walk diagonally left from the station entrance and go up the road facing you to reach the Safeway car park. Walk through this and along the left-hand side of the store. Turn left along an alleyway, through a car park, then reaching a road at Monkmoor Court turn right. ✲ At the road junction continue forward along the pedestrianised Commercial Street: this leads into High Town. Look out for Lloyds-TSB Bank on the right-hand side, then on the opposite side of the road look for a alleyway signed 'To the Cathedral and Church Street' to reach the starting point of Hereford Cathedral.

Bus: Arriving by bus go to the western end of the bus station, turn right, then left along the main road and pick up instructions for train travellers at ✲ above.

Return:

From the Cathedral retrace your steps along Church Street (opposite the north side of the cathedral), cross a road to get back to High Town, turn right, then fork left and cross the main road. Then turn right opposite the Merton Hotel for the bus station or continue for about 25 metres to take the easily missed path at Monkmoor Court, pass a parking area and turn right to fork left over the Safeway car park to reach the station.

From The Victory (omitting the cathedral) turn right after leaving the pub, cross the road and go left along Turner Street. Cross Central Avenue and swing left along St Guthlac Street. At the T-junction turn right, then left. A car park and the bus station are on the right. Continue forward past this to reach the main road, turn right for a few metres and then left at Monkmoor Court to follow the path back to the railway station.

15

Ancient Steps and a Leaning Tower

Bridgnorth

Special Features: Severn Valley Railway trip to Hampton Loade; Hampton Loade Ferry; Castle Hill Railway; Bridgnorth Castle and many other historic features in Bridgnorth; Bridgnorth town trail. Possible diversion to visit Dudmaston Hall (NT).

Distance: A: 11.75 km/7½ miles; B (Town trail): About 4 km/2½ miles. The two walks can be combined.

Start: A: Bridgnorth Station (Severn Valley Railway) (GR716926); B: North Gate at the far (northern) end of High Street (GR719934).

Maps: Explorer 218; Landranger 138; Town map, available from the Tourist Office.

Car Parking: Bridgnorth Station (Severn Valley Railway) car park (GR716926); Car park a little further north from North Gate at the junction with Innage Lane (GR715935).

Public Transport: 1) Severn Valley Railway from Kidderminster. 2) Bus service 890 from Wolverhampton to Bridgnorth. Alight at Bridgnorth Station for the A walk, near to North Gate for the B walk. Return buses leave from High Street at the stop between North Gate and the Town Hall

Terrain: A: Undulating. One quite steep descent and an optional climb up 200+ steps in Bridgnorth. Otherwise nothing severe. Several woodlands, field paths and riversides; B: Quite strenuous with several sets of steps to ascend and descend.

Refreshments: Pub at Hampton Loade; numerous pubs, teashops and restaurants in Bridgnorth.

Notes: 1) At the time of publication the ferry runs April–Mid-July weekends and bank holidays only, then daily 10 am-6 pm to mid-September

2) If you wish to do the A walk when the railway and/or the ferry is not operating you can start from Hampton Loade by using the 297 bus service (Bridgnorth/Kidderminster). Leave the bus about 1.5 km/just under a mile south of Quatt (GR761868) and walk down the lane signed Hampton Loade to reach the River Severn and pick up the walk from the ferry landing point.

3) Another alternative is to use the railway but then walk back to Bridgnorth following a section of the Severn Way. This route is described on page 110.

The Pubs

Railwayman's Arms, Platform One, Severn Valley Railway Station **(GBG)**
This occupies the original licensed refreshment room. It is described in the *Good Beer Guide* as a characterful, charismatic drinking spot and a must for beer drinkers and steam railway enthusiasts. Note the superb Cheshire's Brewery (Smethwick) mirror above the welcoming coal fireplace. Good cask ales, some from local breweries. Traditional cider.

Friars Inn, St Mary's Street **(GBG)**
One of the oldest inns in Bridgnorth, attractively situated in a quiet street and accessed through an archway. A Grade II listed building and a former posting house. Good cask ales including some guest ales.

For the B walk (Town Trail) go to page 110

A walk

Take the Severn Valley Railway train from Bridgnorth station and alight at Hampton Loade. Go down to the road and turn right along it to reach the river and enter a camping ground. The ferry is just on the right with a bell to call the ferryman. Cross the river, walk up to the car park and turn left through a kissing gate. However, if you want some refreshment before starting your walk back to Bridgnorth the River and Rail Country Inn is a short distance away to your right. After going through the kissing gate walk along the side of the River Severn towards a South Staffs

Bridgnorth station

waterworks access bridge. Just before you reach this cross a stile and a footbridge and swing right to go under the bridge and reach another stile about 35 metres to the left of the near right-hand corner of the field.

Cross the stile and walk up into woodland. After about 100 metres the path splits: here take the left fork and follow the undulating path along Long Covert. Ignore a path going off to the left and just after reaching the highest point pass a track coming in from the right. Now descend, soon with steps and with a pool on the right. *When I first walked this section in spring wild flowers were abundant and very beautiful.* Cross three footbridges, two wooden and one brick, and ascend. Then, just before reaching a wicket gate, branch left up steps and turn left

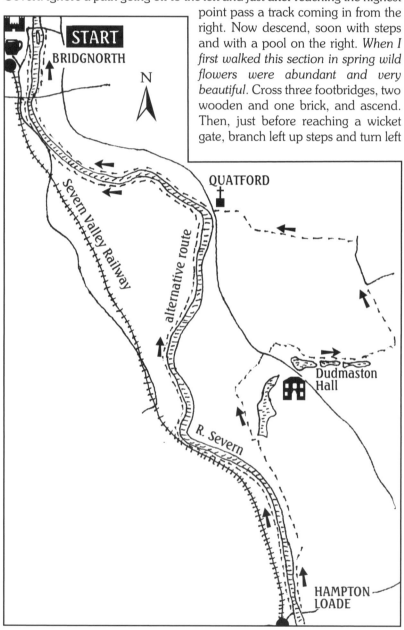

to very shortly cross a stile into a field and go forward to the corner of a fence with a group of large trees a little further on.

At the fence turn right along a gravelled track passing Dudmaston Big Pool to your right. Dudmaston Hall (NT) soon comes into view beyond the pool though this is rather hidden when trees are in leaf. After passing Lodge Farm on your left turn right along tarmac towards woodland ahead. Reaching a road turn right for about 30 metres, then cross to go up a few steps and go diagonally right along a National Trust permissive footpath to reach a track coming up from the road. *If you want to add a visit to the seventeenth century Dudmaston Hall with its magnificent lakeside gardens (01764 780866 for opening times) just continue along the road for about a kilometre to reach the entrance.*

Turn left along the track, soon passing a National Trust waymarked path on the right. Cross a forestry track, very soon followed by another, and about 20 metres further on turn right along a waymarked path. After passing an area of young trees on your left turn left along another waymarked path. On meeting a forestry barrier on your right go through a gap in the rails. Turn right and after about 100 metres reach a seat under a tree and a junction of tracks. Walk to the right of the seat and go forward to join a farm track along the right-hand edge of a field with woodland on the right.

Follow the farm track passing a large pig farm and ignoring a left fork to reach Little Mose Farm. Here turn left along a road and follow this for about 400 metres to reach a gate (or a hedge gap) on the left opposite a waymarked track on the right and about 75 metres after an S-bend in the road. Go through the gate and walk straight forward across the field towards a protruding corner of woodland. Cross a stile at the corner into the woodland. Go forward, swinging left after about 100 metres and following National Trust waymark signs. Cross a forestry track and very soon descend steeply to cross another track. Now follow the meandering path, passing a left fork near a National Trust waymark sign, until it reaches a field a few metres to the right and swings left. Here leave the path and cross a stile on the right and go forward across two fields to reach Hillhouse Farm.

Turn left along concrete, passing a waymarked stile on your right and the farmhouse on your left and continue along a stony track, soon descending along tarmac. Swing left through a sandstone cutting to pass on your right the Church of St Mary Magdalene, Quatford (the church is normally locked but the churchyard is well worth a visit). Continue down to the main road and turn right along this. After about 100 metres fork right along the old road to Bridgnorth and follow it down to reach the main road again. Turn right along this for a few metres and then, by a bus stop, cross the road very carefully and take a footpath to the right of Rock Cottage that leads you down to the River Severn. Cross a stile and now follow a pleasant riverside path for about 3.25km/2 miles back to Bridgnorth. Just after starting along the river you may be able to see Quatford Castle through the trees on the high ground over to the right.

As you pass a mobile homes park on the other side of the river you can see ahead the remains of Bridgnorth Castle, the domed tower of St Mary Magdalene Church and the spire of St Leonard's Church. Approaching Bridgnorth go through a caravan park and pass under the A458, then after about another 500 metres follow a side channel of the river to the bridge that separates High Town from Low Town. Go up steps to the road.

If you have travelled by bus and wish to miss out High Town turn right for the bus stop in Low Town.

Continuing to High Town turn left across the bridge and cross the B4363 very carefully to reach the Castle Hill railway where you can ascend to High Town.

✪ *Severn route joins here.*

However, you may like to climb the Stoneway steps for the experience – it's not too difficult (honest!). Once used by horses they are just to the left of the railway entrance – and there are only 137 steps! En route you pass the unique Theatre on the Steps.

The Castle Hill Railway *was opened in 1892 and was a great boon to residents who previously had had a steep climb to reach High Town. A survey in 1890 counted over 3000 people doing this in twelve hours. The slope of railway the track is 33 degrees, making it the steepest in England.*

Bridgnorth Castle

Ancient Steps and a Leaning Tower

Leaving the upper station, or the steps, turn left to walk around Castle Hill with a fine view of the Severn Valley below. Pass the church of St Mary Magdalene and a large white house to reach a gate that will take you into the Castle gardens and, after passing an impressive war memorial, to the Castle ruins.

Bridgnorth Castle was built in the twelfth century but by the early sixteenth century had partly fallen into ruin, no longer having the same strategic importance that it had had when it was built and much of its stonework having been taken by local residents for building. It regained some importance during the Civil War when a Royalist regiment was stationed in the town, although their bad behaviour prompted many complaints from residents.

In 1646 Bridgnorth came under attack by Roundhead troops and much of the town was destroyed. The castle surrendered in April and the town was handed over to the Parliamentary forces. Because of its hazardous state the demolition of the castle was ordered and little exists today other than parts of the wall and the remains of the Great Tower which leans at an angle of 17 degrees – greater than the Leaning Tower of Pisa!

A country-wide collection for the repair of the town was held in 1648, with a second collection in 1661, after the restoration of the monarchy.

Walk to the right of the castle ruins and follow a brick path to a T-junction, then turn right to reach the church of St Mary Magdalene.

The Church of St Mary Magdalene. A chapel to Mary Magdalene was first dedicated on this site in the twelfth century with the building of the castle. The fourteenth century chapel was demolished in 1792 and the present church was constructed 1792-1796, the architect being Thomas Telford. It is a strikingly beautiful building and is well worth a visit.

Now return to the T-junction and go straight forward towards a car parking area, then turn right along West Castle Street to reach High Street.

If you want to combine this walk with the B walk (Town trail) continue along High Street to North Gate and now read from page 110.

Our main route now turns left along Listley Street but you may first like to continue along High Street to see the striking Town Hall (see page 113) in the centre of the street. This was built after the Civil War and completed in 1652.

Bus travellers may wish to end their walk at the bus stop just beyond the Town Hall near Barclay's Bank.

Now retrace your steps to Listley Street (signed 'To the Railway Station') and turn down this. Immediately before reaching the Library and Tourist Information Centre turn left down steps – though you may like to first go into the Tourist Information Centre to collect more information about the town and its many sites of interest. The steps lead you into the steeply descending Railway Street with its many attractive cottages, then at the T-junction turn left to reach the station car park and the end of the walk.

Severn Way route

From Hampton Loade station go down to the road and turn right along it to reach the river and enter a camping ground. The ferry across the river is just on the right with a bell to call the ferryman. Continue forward through the camping ground and follow the river, soon going under a bridge leading to a Severn-Trent waterworks access bridge. After going through several fields (and noting that many of the stiles hereabouts were made in nearby Dudmaston) the path descends nearer to the river to go along the edge of woodland.

Reaching the hamlet of Lower Forge pass a flood level board and walk with houses and a fine outcrop of sandstone on the left. Continuing through fields see, on the other side of the river, a caravan park, a high sandstone cliff with oaks growing precariously on it, and then the village of Quatford. Soon, on the left is Cliff Coppice that we meet to walk beside its edge. Across the river the church of St Mary Magdalene, high above Bridgnorth, comes into view.

After crossing a stile and passing a 'Private' notice the path goes between trees and swings away from the river to reach a road. *On the opposite side of the road is **Daniel's Mill**, a working corn mill with the largest waterwheel still in use in England. It is open weekends and Wednesdays 2-4pm, Easter to September, and Bank Holiday Mondays 2-6pm Wholemeal flour can be purchased. (For more information phone 01746 762753.)*

Continue along the path which rejoins the river. After crossing a stile and entering a meadow you have a choice – to return directly to Bridgnorth station or to continue along the river and join up with the main walk into High Town. If you make the latter choice carry on beside the river to reach Bridgnorth bridge (*see page 115*) and here leave the river and cross a road, *very carefully*, to reach the Cliff Railway where you can ascend to High Town. Now continue reading from ✪ on page 108.

Otherwise, fork left towards the left-hand end of the road bridge ahead and here cross a stile and turn right along a road (very carefully, because it can be rather busy). Immediately go under the A458 and then, just after passing the B4368 joining from the right, leave the road to ascend steps to the station and the end of the walk.

B walk (Town Trail)

The North Gate is the only gate remaining from the medieval town walls. It was originally constructed of wood but has been largely rebuilt. The site dates back to the eleventh century. It now houses the

Northgate Museum which contains a fine collection of town artefacts: open Easter to October, Sats, Suns and Bank Holidays; Mons, Tues, Weds in School Hols, 11am-4pm, Sats 2pm-4pm. On the northern side of the gate are some attractive seventeenth century houses along an alley on the left.

After reading the 'Memorandum' on North Gate (describing the disastrous fire that almost completely destroyed High Town in 1649) walk along High Street immediately passing on the left the seventeenth century Golden Lion Inn. *This was a coaching inn and the old entrance to the stables can be seen to the left. The mounting block for customers to mount their horses is still in existence at the front of the building.* Go along High Street for about 50 metres and turn right into Whitburn Street to view on the right the timber framed and gabled King's Head. The Crown opposite dates from 1646. Then return to High Street and cross it into Church Street shortly passing old almshouses on the left with a little garden beside them. The almshouses were founded in the reign of Henry VI and were partly damaged by enemy action in 1940 and rebuilt 1950. A cottage beside them was also damaged and the ground has been converted into a garden of remembrance.

You then reach St Leonard's Close and St Leonard's Church (now no longer used for worship), situated on the highest point of the town and a prominent landmark visible from the river on the main walk.

St Leonard's Church. *The first church here was built before 1250 but the present building is largely Victorian. On 31 March 1646, during the Civil War, the Royalist Commander Colonel Billingsley was killed in the church. The Parliamentarians then used the church as an ammunition store but it was hit by Royalist cannon fire from Panpudding Hill (near the Railway Station). The explosion of the gunpowder and the consequent blaze destroyed much of the church and the town's records and spread beyond the church to most of High Town, rendering almost 300 families homeless and destitute. St Leonard's was partially rebuilt in 1662. Outside the church is the remains of an old church cross. The church is open to the public daily, April to September.*

Walk clockwise around the Close keeping to the road nearest to the church. You first pass Richard Baxter's House: *'the learned and eloquent Richard Baxter' was a prominent Puritan who lived here 1640-1641 and was a curate of St Leonard's. He then moved to Kidderminster where he spent some fifteen years of his life, first as a lecturer and later vicar. He was ejected from Kidderminster following the restoration of Charles II and spent the rest of his life in and around London, preaching and writing, but often suffering persecution and imprisonment because of his faith.*

Next pass on your left the building that originally housed the old grammar school: *this was founded here in 1503, originally occupying a former chapel. It was replaced by the present building in 1785, the school moving into new premises in Bridgnorth in 1909.*

After passing St Leonard's House there is a fine view across the Severn Valley. You then reach the building, originally three cottages, that housed the grammar school, the school master, and the vicar of St Leonard's. *Note the windows with stone mullions and the attractive and diagonally set chimneystacks. After the school moved to the building passed earlier the cottages were converted into school dormitories.* To the left are the Granary Steps and I suggest that you continue your walk down these and then return by ascending another set of steps. However, if you prefer something less strenuous just go past the house to the top of St Leonard's Steps and then continue reading from ★ below.

Richard Baxter's House (centre)

Feeling sufficiently energetic walk down the Granary Steps (88 steps). They are one of seven sets of ancient steps that connect High Town, set on a 100 foot high sandstone cliff, to the river and to Low Town. At the bottom of the steps turn right along a road passing Friars Loade and just after passing a parking area (where there is seating and another fine view across the Severn Valley) and meeting Cartway on the left turn right through an easily missed archway (to the right of house 69) and ascend the St Leonard's Steps . On reaching St Leonard's Close again, turn left.

★ Almost immediately pass the almshouses of Palmer's Hospital Charity. *The first houses were built and endowed in 1687 by Francis Palmer, the rector of Sandy in Bedfordshire, whose mother was buried in the church. She was the sister of the Colonel Billingsley who had been killed in the church. The present houses were re-built in 1889.*

Continue around the close and then return along Church Street to the High Street and turn left. Opposite you will see the NatWest building with three sandstone gargoyles, gargoyle downspouts and the figure of a man carved in the centre. On the main signboard is a small model of the North Gate. Reaching the Town Hall in the centre of the street walk through the archways where you will find two boards listing the many important dates in the history of the town. Opposite are two timber-framed buildings, the one on the left having black rose decorations under the windows. The one on the right has red roses together with the names of six girls under the windows – Holly, Naomi, Robin, Charolette, Emma, Trudi. There seem to be two opinions of the origins of these: 1 – they were the names of the children born to a family living in the building; 2 – they were the names of the various flat holders.

Town Hall. *The original town hall was destroyed in the Civil War and the present timber framed building on a sandstone base (now*

brick faced) was erected after the war and completed in 1652. It is believed to have originally been a barn and bought from nearby Much Wenlock for fifty pounds – though there seem to be some doubts about this. Substantial alterations were made in 1887 but the interior has been carefully preserved and contains historical material relating to the town: it is at times open to the public.

On leaving the Town Hall note the old drinking fountain on the end of the building. On the right is St Mary's Street, one of three streets off High Street, which formed the planned new town of the mid-twelfth century. The other streets are Whitburn Street and Listley Street, but St Mary's

Bridgnorth Town Hall

113

Street is the best preserved. About 50 metres down the street on the right is the Friars Inn. There is also a number of good timber framed buildings; side passages once led to workshops, stables and cottages for the servants.

Continuing past the Town Hall, on the left is The Swan, a mid-seventeenth century coaching inn with yard behind. Opposite is the timber framed Tanner's Wine Shop. This is decorated with four Tudor figures. The most provocative is that of a woman with her skirt pulled up above her knee! They are thought to have been on an earlier building in Bridgnorth and were found in a merchant's yard and added to this building in the nineteenth century.

At the end of High Street meet Waterloo Terrace and here turn left along Cartway, at one time the only route by which carts could bring goods from the river wharfs up to High Town. Extra horses were needed for stagecoaches. At the top of Cartway was Cowgate, one of the original five town gates. Traces of the gate can be seen in the wall of a building opposite Waterloo Terrace.

Walk down Cartway and just before reaching a T-junction you will see on the left the remains of cave houses that were used as family dwellings until 1856. Follow Cartway as it turns right, passing on the left Bank Steps, then the Black Boy Inn, a seventeenth century listed building.

Black Boy Inn. *The name honoured the restoration of Charles II who had a dark complexion and was known as 'the black boy'. This is the last remaining ale house of the twenty or so originally in Cartway. Many of the attractive cottages in the road were once boarding houses or ale houses – or worse! – used by sailors, traders*

Bridgnorth Bridge

and visitors from the bustling river port. It was an area with a rather dingy reputation!

On the left meet Bishop Percy's House, now occupied by Bridgnorth Boy's Club. *This was built in 1580 and is one of the few timber framed buildings that survived the fire of 1646. It is named after Dr. Percy, the Bishop of Dromore in Northern Ireland who was born here in 1729. He was largely responsible for a revival of interest in medieval poetry in the eighteenth century.* Next to Bishop Percy's House is Ashwood Loade, with a front garden on the street. According to a plaque on the wall the garden was created by the owner Mr Ashwood in 1940 who, since 1988, 'smiles down from above'. Past this is the Bassa Villa Bar, dated 1591. As described on the wall, Bassa Villa means 'basin of the town', later changed to 'Lower Town' and now known as 'Low Town'. Just beyond on the right is the sixteenth century Bridgend Cottage carrying an old fire insurance sign and some horse brasses and horseshoes. Very shortly pass on the left Bridgnorth Bridge.

Bridgnorth Bridge. *The first bridge was probably constructed here in Saxon times but the first definite record of one is in 1272. The present structure was designed by Thomas Telford and built in 1823. At the far end is a clock tower and this carries an inscription commemorating the building of the first steam locomotive in a nearby foundry in 1808. In the seventeenth century the Severn was one of the busiest rivers in Europe.*

Pass the Cliff Railway met on the main walk (see page 108), and then, a few metres after passing a postbox situated on the other side of the road, turn right to ascend St Mary's Steps (99 steps) to reach Castle Walk, said by Charles I to give 'the finest view in my domain'. *Across from here you can see Panpudding Hill from where the Royalist canon fired on the castle.* Turn right, then left up more steps to St Mary's Church. This magnificent building (*visited on the main walk – see page 109*) was built by Thomas Telford of engineering fame. Opposite the church entrance turn right into Castle East Street, shortly passing on the right the Governor's House, originally the home of the Castle Governor. This is in a similar style to the three cottages in St Leonard's Close that contained the clergy's and schoolmaster's houses and was built around the same time. Charles I visited here twice when the house was the Royalist headquarters for Shropshire. Most of the other houses in the street are late Georgian. Look back a good view of the square tower of St Mary's Church.

Now turn right along High Street to reach the Museum of Childhood and Costume and the site of the Postern Gate. The museum (open daily 10.30am–5pm) contains a costume gallery and a complete Victorian nursery. It is housed in New Market Buildings, constructed – somewhat incongruously – in Italianate style in 1855. It was intended to house street traders, but they resisted the move. Turn left along Listley Street with the museum on the left carrying an old sign pointing to the railway station. This will take you to the library and tourist office, opposite a car park and toilets. Immediately before the library turn left to descend steeply along Railway Street, passing some attractive cottages. At the bottom turn left – for the railway station if you have left your car there – otherwise, ascend steps, cross New Road and ascend more steps, then turn right to enter the castle grounds. Ahead is the War Memorial but turn left to walk around the castle remains (see page 108), turn left again to join a car park, then right to pass several pubs and reach High Street and the end of your tour. The bus stop is past the Town Hall, on the right near Barclay's Bank.

16

A Royalist Stronghold

Ludlow

Special Features: Ludlow Castle; St Laurence's Church; Ludlow Museum; Whitcliffe Common.

Distance: A: 13 km/8 miles ; B: 9.5 km/6 miles. The A and B walks link at two points, so enabling you to combine part of each to produce a walk of intermediate length.

Starting point: Ludlow, Castle Square (GR509746).

Maps: Explorer 203; Landranger 137.

Car Parking: Pay and Display car park off Castle Square (GR509746). Walk up to the square and turn left.

Public transport: Rail and bus services to Ludlow. From the **Railway Station** turn left and walk uphill. Approaching a T-junction turn right and go through a car park, leaving it by a gate to reach the rear of the Feathers Hotel. Here swing left to meet a 'Walkway to the Town' beside the Feathers and follow this to Corve Street (where **buses stop**). Cross the road, turn left for a few metres and take a passageway on the right, then turn right along King Street. At a road junction turn right along a paved path signed Parish Church, now joining the route starting from the car park. *The walkway beside the Feathers is open 9am to 5pm so if it is closed when you return just carry on down Corve Street and turn right beside the Tesco car park to reach the station.*

Refreshments: Pubs, restaurants and teashops in Ludlow. Ludlow has a high reputation for its food shops and restaurants..

Terrain: A strenuous ascent into the Mortimer Forest but otherwise nothing too difficult along paths and quiet lanes through fields and some beautiful woodlands. About half a mile of road walking towards the end of walk A, but there is a good pavement.

The Pubs

Many of the Ludlow pubs look promising. Two very good ones that I have used are: **The Charlton Arms Hotel (GBG)** (A walk only) near Ludford Bridge, a former coaching inn; and the fourteenth century **Church Inn (GBG)** in Church Street. Both have a good selection of cask ales including a number of local brews. The Church Inn has a very interesting collection of old cameras, rather tucked away in a corner.

Leaving the car park turn left in Castle Square to enter the narrow Castle Street. Just past the Church Inn turn left, signed 'Parish Church', to reach St Lawrence's Church.

St Laurence's Church *is the largest parish church in Shropshire and cathedral-like in character. It was given five stars by Simon Jenkins in*

his book England's Thousand Best Churches. *St Laurence's dates from 1199 with much rebuilding in the fourteenth and fifteenth centuries. Most impressive is the fifteenth century chancel with sixteenth and seventeenth century tombs and with windows depicting the story*

One of the misericords in the Church of St Lawrence

of St Laurence. Especially interesting are the fifteenth century misericords on the priest's stalls with heraldic devices and scenes of everyday life. St John's Chapel contains two magnificent windows; in the North Transept is a 1764 four-manual organ. The lantern

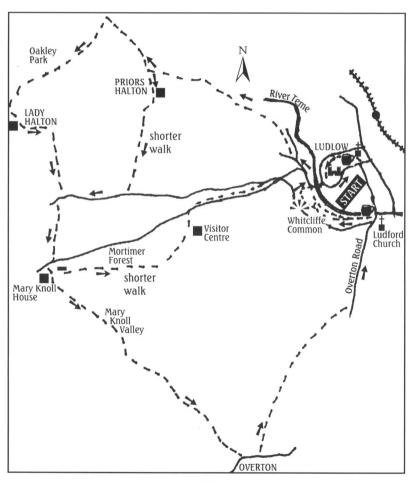

tower contains eight bells and provides good views of the town and the surrounding countryside. One of the glories of the church is the wooden vault above the stone lantern. The Lady Chapel once housed the town fire engine and the wooden pegs that held the fire buckets remain. The Jesse Window is fourteenth century, though much restored. Near the North Door is a memorial to the poet A E Housman, author of A Shropshire Lad.

Turn left in front of the church along a narrow passageway, then turn right to pass Hosyers Almshouse, originally built in 1486 and rebuilt in 1758. At a T-junction turn left and, reaching a road, walk to the left of this along a raised walkway, soon passing beside the walls of Ludlow Castle and following a short section of the Mortimer Trail.

Ludlow Castle *pre-dates the town and was built between 1086 and 1094 and has been much extended. It was owned by the Mortimer family in the fourteenth century and then passed to the House of York after Edward IV's victory at the Battle of Mortimer's Cross in 1461, an important event in the Wars of the Roses. It was a Royalist stronghold in the Civil War but surrendered to the Parliamentary forces after a siege of thirty-three days in 1646.*

At a fork in the path go right and descend to join a road, then turn right to cross Dinham Bridge. Follow the road round to the right and at a Y-junction, continue forward along a No Through Road, signed Priors Halton.

Just before reaching the Cliffe Hotel go through a kissing-gate on the right and walk forward, gradually moving over towards the trees on the right and leave the field by a stile and a footbridge in the far right corner. Immediately take a stile on the left and turn right to walk beside the trees again. Through the trees are views of the river and the Teme valley although these can only be seen intermittently when the trees are in leaf. Cross a stile into a second field and look back for a good view of the castle.

Almost at the end of the field turn left at a waymark post, leave the field by a stile and descend to another waymark post. Continue your descent through trees, cross a footbridge and a stile and walk diagonally across the field to leave it in its far right corner. Cross a stile and continue diagonally across the next field, leaving this also in its far right corner. Follow a short farm track through a gate to reach tarmac.

Here the A & B walks make a first separation. For the longer A walk continue reading from ✪ *on page 120.*

Following the B walk turn left to pass a farm and go through the hamlet of Priors Halton. On the left is a good view of Titterstone Clee and you may be able to spot the tower of Ludlow Church. Just past the last of farm buildings turn right along a waymarked track and follow this to reach a road. Turn right along this, good views of Wenlock Edge and the Long

Mynd opening up to the right as the road ascends. After about 600 metres meet a track coming in on the right along which the A walk joins. *Now continue reading from* ★ *below.*

✪ Continuing the A walk turn right and follow the switchback lane, passing an attractive stone-built cottage and going through woodland. Pass a road gate and about 100 metres after starting to descend meet a waymark post on the right and turn left along a lane bordered by recently planted oaks. Reaching an old metal barn on the left pass a line of oaks marking Duchess Walk in Oakley Park, once owned by Clive of India. Follow the road for about another 500 metres to pass houses on the right and a barn on the left. Turn left beside the barn, then right to follow a stony track to pass more barns on the right, go through a gate and turn left along a grassy track. Descend to cross a stream, ascend to reach a house on the left, then turn right for about 50 metres to go through a bridleway gate beside a metal farm gate and descend between fences. Continue to reach a road, going through another bridleway gate en route and turn right, now joining the shorter route.

★ The road swings left and now, very shortly, turn left through a bridleway gate and ascend steeply to enter the Mortimer Forest (*where I gorged myself on blackberries*). Continue to ascend, cross a forestry track, and soon join a road. Here turn right and after about 50 metres turn left through a bridleway gate to reach, after another 50 metres, a Y-junction of paths.

Here the A and B walks separate again. For walk B continue reading from ✳ *on page 122.*

Continuing walk A take the right fork to pass houses on the right and descend through woodland, very shortly swinging left through a gate to leave the woodland and descend steeply. Soon re-enter woodland to walk down the Mary Knoll Valley where, if you are lucky, you may see a unique herd of shaggy fallow deer. As you descend you will pass a series of numbered posts (a forestry trail) and at No. 26 (*Trails are sometimes re-routed and the posts renumbered*) cross a forestry track and continue forward. A little further on pass a seat on the right and then, reaching a forestry road where it makes a U-bend, continue forward along this, passing a house on the right. Pass another forestry road on the right and leave the Forestry Commission land (Sunny Dingle) by a traffic barrier and soon join a road.

Turn left along this, passing an old parish milepost showing 'Ludlow 2 miles and Lemster (*sic*) 8 miles'. Follow this road for about 150 metres and then turn left along what looks like a private drive (it is a right of way). Leave the lane at a T-junction and continue forward across grass and cross a stile beside a gate. Now go through two fields with a hedge on the right and with good views of Titterstone Clee. Cross a stile into a third field, now with a hedge on the left, soon joining another field with a hedge on the right and leaving this along an enclosed track. Continue through a field, leave it by a stile to pass through a patch of woodland and reach the B4361.

Turn left and follow the road for about half a mile/a kilometre (there is a good pavement) to approach traffic lights and Ludford Bridge. Here you have a choice. For refreshment the Charlton Arms Hotel is just ahead. To visit Ludford Church turn right along Park Road, then right into the churchyard. Otherwise turn left for a few metres (or right if you are returning from the hotel and/or the church) and go up steps on the right to enter Whitcliffe Common, passing an information board.

Ludford Church. The settlement of Ludford predates Ludlow and St Giles' Church is thought to date back to the twelfth century on the evidence of a Norman window in the west end. This pre-dates the addition of the tower in, probably, the fifteenth century. However, little is known of the early history of the church and extensive changes were made in the mid-nineteenth century. The south door was only added in 1949 and is on the site of the original medieval door. There is a medieval entrance into the chancel The chapel on the north side is sixteenth century and contains some fine brasses and tombs: the tomb of Sir Job Charlton is particularly impressive.

Whitcliffe Common forms part of what was a much larger medieval common and is an area of great interest to geologists because of the pioneering studies that the nineteenth century geologist Sir Roderick Murchison carried out here, work which helped to overturn the then currently held view that the fossil record was evidence of divine creation. The Ludlow rocks contain the marine fossils on which he based his work: in 1839 he named these the Ludlow Rocks of the Silurian System. Darwin's Origin of Species was published twenty years later in 1859. There is a very informative section in the Ludlow Museum devoted to Murchison's work in the area. Part of the common is a Site of Special Scientific Interest. If you want to study the geology in more detail you can obtain a leaflet describing a Teme Bank Trail from the Tourist Office in Castle Square. You may be able to find some fossils, though I was unsuccessful.

As the common is of such interest I have given three possible routes through it, 1) being the shortest and 3) being the longest and highest and providing the best views.

Walk straight forward along what is known as the Bread Walk, so named because it was constructed by the poor and unemployed who were paid for their labours in bread. *You have a good view of Ludlow and the castle, and below is the River Teme.*

At a Y-junction of paths you have the first choice of routes that will take you back to Dinham Bridge.

1)   Take the right fork and continue along the Bread Walk, descend and pass a weir to reach Dinham Bridge. *Continue from* 🌸 *on page 123.*

2)   Take the left fork and ascend to pass a stone seat on the right where there is a good view of the castle. Pass through a grassy area and walk along the edge of Whitcliffe Woods. Reaching another grassy area with a seat on the right giving a good view over Ludlow you now have another choice of routes.

2)   (*contd*) Pass the seat to descend through woodland and at a T-junction of paths turn right and descend further, with a good view of the castle, to Dinham Bridge. *Continue from* 🌸 *on page 123.*

3)   Fork left and ascend. *On your left, in the woodland, you will see the remains of a number of earthworks which are thought to have been cut during the Civil War by the Parliamentary forces for artillery to be used against the Royalist garrison in Ludlow. However, the guns were not needed and Ludlow surrendered on 1 June 1646.* At a Y-junction of paths fork right to enter open common. Here turn right and descend through woodland. Reaching a crossing path turn left along this to ascend, pass the common just met, soon having another excellent view of the castle. Follow the path until you reach a T-junction of paths, with a seat on the right, and here turn right to descend, with two sets of steps, to reach Dinham Bridge. *Continue from* 🌸 *on page 123.*

✳ *Walk B.*

Take the left fork to pass a barn and after about 50 metres go through a bridleway gate on the left and turn right to walk along a sunken track with a hedge on the right. Go through a gate, with a stile and gate on the left, and continue forward along the track (*more blackberries*). After this swings right to meet a gate take a path on the left of the gate and enter woodland. Meeting a path coming in from the right join it for a few metres and then, as it swings left, leave it to continue forward along a grassy path. *After passing a track coming in from the right you will soon be walking on Ludlow rocks (see p 121, Whitcliffe Common); these can be very slippery when wet.*

When you meet a main forestry track turn left along it to pass the Visitor Centre on your right and reach a road. Cross this to enter woodland, passing a forest track on your left, and take a path on your left signed 'Ludlow 1 mile'. Follow this for a few metres, then turn right, waymarked 'Mortimer Trail, permissive path', and follow the undulating path to eventually join a road. At a road junction take the right fork and ascend, soon walking with Whitcliffe Common (*see page 121*) on the left. At a T-junction turn left, then almost immediately left again and leave the road at a fine viewpoint to walk down to an information board/toposcope.

Turn right and walk past several seats, then descend beside bracken to enter Whitcliffe Woods. Continue your descent and reaching a crossing

Looking across to Ludlow Castle

path turn right along this. Enter a grassy area and turn left along a descending path, then at a T-junction of paths turn right, the river soon appearing below. The Ludlow Rocks are much in evidence here as you descend to reach Dinham Bridge.

❋ Cross the bridge and ascend, with the walls of Ludlow Castle on the left. Pass, on the right, the twelfth century Chapel of St Thomas, Ludlow's oldest building other than the castle. Reaching steps on the left go up these and turn right to walk around the castle walls. To your right, across the road is the fine, half-timbered 2 Dinham, rebuilt in 1656 after having been burnt in the Civil War. It is worth going across to this to admire the beautifully carved timber-work. Continue to the castle entrance.

Leaving the castle go forward into Castle Square, passing a Russian canon, captured by British forces in 1855 during the Crimean War. Walk along the left of the square to reach the car park, or a little further along Church Street for the Church Inn and/or the Church of St Lawrence. On the right-hand side of the square is the Museum and Tourist Information Centre. *For trains and buses continue into King Street, turn left into Corve Street and, for the station, retrace your steps from The Feathers.*

Ludlow Museum. *Although only a small museum this is well worth a visit, especially if you have an interest in geology since it has a section devoted to the work of Sir Roderick Murchison (see Whitcliffe Common, page 121).*

17

The Firing of the Industrial Revolution

Ironbridge and Benthall Woods

Special Features: The Iron Bridge, Toll House Museum, Benthall Hall and gardens (NT), The Boat Inn.

Distance: A: 10.25 km/6½ miles; B: 5 km/3¼ miles.
Start: Ironbridge High Street (GR671035).
Maps: Explorer 242; Landranger 127.
Car Parking: Pay & Display car park close to the Iron Bridge (GR673033) on the south side of the river. Also other car parks in Ironbridge. If you use the park on the south side leave it near the Iron Bridge and cross the road towards the sign to Benthall Edge picnic site. Then start reading from the fourth sentence of the instructions on page 125.
Public Transport: See box on page 130.
Terrain: Undulating with one steep climb. Woodland, riverside and field paths with some good views. Some paths may be quite muddy in wet periods.
Refreshments: The Boat Inn, Coalport; Pubs and teashops in Ironbridge.

The Pub

The Boat Inn, Coalport

The Boat Inn was first licensed in 1831 but before this it was used as a refuge in bad weather for workers from Broseley using the nearby ferry (now replaced by the fine bridge that you can see to the right) to reach the Coalport china works. (You can visit the China Museum on walk no 18.) This was probably the biggest producer of china in England and most of the families in Broseley had members working there. In 1799 there was a major disaster when the ferryboat capsized and 28 people drowned.

The inn is no stranger to flooding as you will see from the flood level board outside. It is a substantially built structure and has survived perhaps 200 floodings. Inside is much industrial memorabilia relating to the area with some interesting historical photographs, one showing the opening of the bridge in 1920. Look also for one showing the pub in one of its periodic immersions. Food and the usual Banks's cask ales.

The Firing of the Industrial Revolution

The Iron Bridge. *The spectacular Severn Gorge is rich in coal, iron-ore, clay and limestone, all the raw materials necessary for industrial development. In 1709, a Quaker ironmaster, Abraham Darby I (the first of four members of a family who bore the same name) invented a technique for cheap iron production using coke instead of charcoal. This gave rise to the Industrial Revolution and the Coalbrookdale area became one of the most important industrialised areas in the world.*

The rapid growth of industry and the consequent increase in industrial traffic soon led to a demand for a new bridge over the River Severn. The river was itself unreliable and there were problems with ferries and in 1776 an Act of Parliament authorised the construction of a bridge, work on which began in 1777. It was the first in the world to use cast-iron structurally, the single arch avoiding the need for piers that would have obstructed traffic. The work was carried out by Abraham Darby III, probably at a furnace about a mile away, although the exact site is unknown.

An exhibition illustrating the history of the bridge is located in the original tollhouse at the south end of the bridge. The tollhouse also houses the Tourist Information Centre.

L eave Ironbridge High Street by crossing the Iron Bridge and passing the old toll house (now one of Ironbridge's nine museums). Look up to the old list of tolls on the wall. Go forward a few metres and turn right towards the Benthall Edge picnic site. However, don't continue along this path but swing left between metal posts towards seats and turn right to now follow the Severn Way, passing under a bridge. The Severn Way

The Iron Bridge

follows the line of the old Severn Valley Railway. Part of this has been restored as a working railway (see Walk 15), but not as far as Ironbridge.

Walk along this attractively tree-lined way for about 450 metres then, just after crossing a bridge (may not be very obvious), turn left on a path that swings right by a waymark, goes through a barrier and ascends steps, now joining the Shropshire Way and very soon crossing a footbridge.

Reaching a junction of paths turn left and ascend more steps, now leaving the Shropshire Way that, initially, follows parallel to our steps. We are here in Benthall Edge Wood in which coal was once mined, probably as long ago as the thirteenth century.

When you pass a quarry (Pattins Rock Quarry) on the left swing right briefly and descend for a few metres, then turn sharp left to ascend by more steps and gain a good view on the left of the quarry from which limestone was once obtained. You also have fine view of Ironbridge.

Leaving the quarry take the right fork, walking, more or less on the level and ignoring all turnings off. The ground soon falls away steeply to the right (Benthall Edge) and some care is needed in places where the path may not be in the best of conditions. A view of Ironbridge power station emerges through the trees.

After about 750 metres and having skirted a quarry on the right turn left to cross a stile beside a gate and go forward along a broad track. After about 500 metres pass Benthall Hall Farm and then, after about another 100 metres take a short track to the left, opposite the entrance to a churchyard, to arrive at St Bartholomews Parish Church, Benthall and the National Trust property of Benthall Hall.

> **Benthall Hall.** *This remarkable sixteenth century house, owned by the National Trust and privately occupied, has a superb interior and some beautiful, carefully restored gardens. The house and gardens are open Wed/Sun/Bank Hol. Mons; 1.30 to 5.30. Admission charge.*
>
> *The adjacent Church of St Bartholomew is of a rather quaint design with an attractive sundial over the original entrance. It was rebuilt after having been damaged during the Civil War. It originally served a small village that lay close to the church but this was destroyed in the Civil War. After the war the cottages were rebuilt nearer to the mines which were then in operation.*

Just past the church turn left through a gate (with an interesting catch) and go straight forward across the field, parallel to the Hall gardens, to reach a gate. Do not go through this but turn right along an avenue of horse chestnuts. Cross a stile and now walk with a fence on the right, shortly passing under power lines. Cross another stile and swing half left, under

Church of St Bartholomew, Benthall; Benthall Hall behind.

power lines again, to walk with a fence on the left, then leave the field by a stile in its far right corner.

Walk with a hedge on the right, soon joining an enclosed track. When this swings right into a farm take a stile on the left and walk across a boggy area past a barn on your right (carefully choosing your steps!) towards a pond. To the right of this cross a stile and turn sharp left along an enclosed path: this joins a tarmac path that takes you down to the road.

Here the A and B walks separate. For the shorter walk B continue reading from ★ on page 130.

Continuing walk A cross the road and go forward along a narrow lane. At a T-junction turn right for a few metres, then turn left along an ascending path, signed Lloyd's Jitty. Cross a lane and ascend a few steps by a telephone box to reach a road. Turn left along this and follow it for about 400 metres, passing a triangular green with a maypole on the left and Broseley Cricket Club on the right. To the left is a good view of the Wrekin. On reaching the last of the housing with 'Woodlands Farmhouse' on the left turn right immediately before 'The Barn' along a path, soon with woodland (Stocking Mound) on your left and the cricket ground on your right.

The path leads into a housing estate where you turn left along Cherrybrook Drive, then on reaching a T-junction turn left with more woodland (Cockshot Mound) on your right. After about 100 metres turn right into Birchmeadow playing fields and turn left to walk around their edge. Just after passing round the second corner go left through a gap in the trees towards a wire fence surrounding a school. Here turn right, passing a large oak and walking across more of the playing fields to pass a children's play area.

Now turn left along Birch Meadow to reach a T-junction. Turn right for about 50 metres and then turn left along a broad path with 'The Downs' on the right. Follow it for about 400 metres to reach the Ironbridge Road. Just before reaching it the path forks left towards a gate. Do not follow this but continue forward over grass to reach the road. Turn right past Tollgate Cottage for a few metres and cross the road to reach a road sign on the left (Broseley. An Early Industrial Town).

Here turn left along a tarmac drive leading to Coneybury Farm and Woodhouse Farm. When the tarmac swings left continue forward, now on a wide track. Go through a gate and continue forward with a hedge on the left, then descend via another gate through woodland (Corbett's Dingle), soon with a stream for company on the right. Pass an impressive sandstone cliff on the left and, on leaving the wood, join a stony drive, then a road and continue downhill to reach the bridge of a dismantled railway that now carries the Severn Valley Way.

Our route now joins this but first you should visit the Boat Inn, if not for refreshment at least to see a building and the surrounding area that has

The Boat Inn

such an interesting history. So to do this continue downhill along the road for about another 100m, passing a road coming in from the left and swinging left to meet the Boat Inn.

This is a delightful spot for wildlife with kingfishers being seen regularly and the occasional otter.

Now return to the bridge, go up the steps and turn left along the Severn Way. (*This section is walked, in the opposite direction, in Walk 18 where some further information is given.*) When you reach a road go forward along the right fork and when this road swings right go forward along a path with the River Severn on the right. Soon ascend to join a road and pass the striking Church of St Mary the Virgin, Jackfield, beautifully patterned with coloured bricks. Swing left, then right to pass, or visit, the Jackfield Tile Museum, the windows appropriately adorned with decorative tiling.

Jackfield Tile Museum is housed in what was originally the tile works of Craven Dunnill, built in 1871. This was a period when many churches were being restored and Craven Dunnill had a good market in decorative floor tiles.

Pass Calcutts Road on the left and Calcutts House to reach Jackfield Sidings and the former level crossing gates.

Calcutts House was built in 1755 by the Ninth Earl of Dundonald, a scientist who invented a method for extracting tar from coal. The house was later occupied by Alexander Brodie, a famous ironmaster

129

whose foundry (now disappeared) filled the combe in front of the house.

Go through a gate to the left of the gates followed by a kissing gate and walk along another attractively wooded section of old railway track, very shortly passing the Black Swan down on the right.

You reach Ironbridge through the car park where you have perhaps left your car. If not continue through the park to the road, turn right to cross the Iron Bridge into the town, the Tontine Hotel facing you.

The Tontine Hotel *was built in 1784 by shareholders of the Iron Bridge and the exterior has changed little since that time. There is a magnificent tile floor in the foyer that was made locally in Jackfield.*

A tontine is an annuity shared by subscribers to an original loan, shares in which increase as the subscribers die, the last survivor receiving all (or until a specified date when those surviving share the proceeds).

★ Continuing the shorter walk B, turn left and follow the road, which descends steeply with a good pavement, and leads back to Ironbridge. Shortly before reaching the town the pavement separates from the road and here you have the choice of two routes. You can either continue along the separated pavement, which now goes beside a stream, then descend steps to reach the Iron Bridge again and your starting point. Alternatively cross the road and go over a stile to enter Benthall Woods again. Follow the path, then at a path junction, where a waymark post points straight ahead, turn right, cross a bridge over your earlier route along the Severn Way and turn right to return to your starting point.

Public Transport to Ironbridge.

Ironbridge is served by buses from Wellington (9, 39, 99), Telford (9, 39, 76, 77, 99), Much Wenlock (39) and Bridgnorth (9, 39). Services 76 and 77 pass the Blists Hill Victorian Town (walk 18) and the Museum of Iron (walk 19). There are rail services to Wellington and Telford Central.

On returning from Ironbridge check the position of the bus stop. From the High Street some buses to Telford leave on the south side of the road, some from the north side! It is best to walk down to the Visitor Centre bus stop (next to the Museum of the Gorge) to avoid this problem.

From Telford Central station allow at least 15 mins to reach the bus station which is reached through the shopping centre. *Do not miss, in Telford Central station, the full-scale replica of the 1803 locomotive, Richard Trevithick. This was the first steam railway locomotive in the world and preceded Stephenson's Rocket by 26 years. The original was built near Ironbridge by the Coalbrookdale Company, 1802-1803.*

18

Life in a Victorian Town

Ironbridge and Blists Hill

Special Features: Blists Hill Museum and Victorian Town, Tile Museum, Maws Craft Centre, Tar Tunnel Museum, Coalport China Museum.

Distance: 7.5km/4¾ miles.
Start: Blists Hill Museum car park (GR695035).
Alternative Start: Ironbridge High Street (GR671035). Start reading from ✪ on page 133.
Maps: Explorer 242; Landranger 127.
Car Parking: Blists Hill Museum (GR695035) or car parks in Ironbridge.
Public Transport: See box on page 130. If starting from Ironbridge start reading from ✪ on page 133.
Refreshments: Blist Hill Victorian Town; All Nations Inn, Blists Hill; Black Swan, Jackfield; Boat Inn, Coalport; The Shakespeare Inn, Coalport; Tar Tunnel Museum Tearooms, Coalport; Tontine Inn and other pubs and teashops in Ironbridge.
Terrain: Hilly. Some fine woodland.

The Pub

The All Nations Inn, Blists Hill. **(GBG)**
Built, as the gable stone indicates, in 1789 it became a beerhouse about 1832. The origin of the unusual name is not known but one possibility is that unused tobacco was mixed in a jar and known as the United Nations Mixture. An account of the history of this traditional and unspoilt inn will be found on the wall to the left of the bar. After having been closed for a couple of years the inn now has, once again, its own brewery and provides good food and local cask ales.

Blists Hill Victorian Town. This occupies the site of the former ironworks and contains reconstructed factories, shops and cottages, designed to illustrate how life was lived in the area in Victorian times.

Leave the car park, pass the Blists Hill Museum on the left, go down to the road (Legges Way) and turn left along it. After just over 100 metres reach a footbridge over the road. Just before reaching it go left up steps and turn right to cross the bridge, then turn right along a road. After a few metres turn sharp left along a driveway, then on reaching a wall turn right to arrive at the All Nations Inn on the right.

Opposite the pub our path goes between a metal pillar and a wall to the left of a gate. However if you first look up beyond metal barriers on the right of the gate you will see the line of a trackway that brought coal and iron ore into the Blists Hill ironworks. Taking our path you will see on the left the old latticework cast iron bridge that originally carried the rails of the trackway.

Descend briefly and swing right, very soon ascend steps (having passed descending steps on the left) and at a waymark post turn left and follow the meandering and undulating path through woodland, carpeted in the spring with wild garlic and bluebells. Emerging from the wood turn left to walk along a stony track with houses on the right. Leaving the housing the track descends, then ascends to soon meet more housing on the right and enters more woodland. Immediately ignoring a path on the left continue forward for a few metres to reach a Y-junction of paths and here take the right fork. After nearly 100 metres reach another Y-junction and take the left fork; the path soon swings right to go beside a fence and a steep drop down into the Severn Gorge on the left, Ironbridge power station soon coming into a view.

Eventually the woodland narrows with housing appearing on the right. After passing fences leave the trees to enter a meadow. Ignore a path going diagonally right towards houses and walk forward, then continue through a second meadow to enter woodland (The Crostan). Turn left here and descend steeply through the woods. After about 200 metres reach a waymark post on the left and a stout seat at a Y-junction of paths. Here turn sharp right, passing the seat. Ascend, and after just over 100 metres ignore an apparent path branching to the right and after another few metres turn left at a waymark post, now descending and meandering around to reach the road. Cross this and go up Harris's Lane opposite.

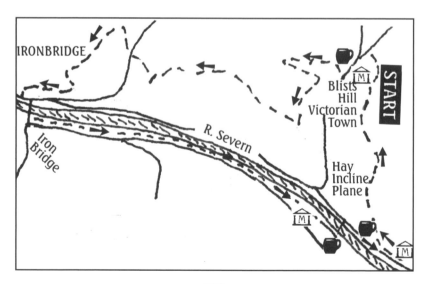

When you reach Roberts Road and housing turn left along a narrow lane between hedges. Pass Orchard Lane on the left and on meeting houses bear right, past a metal gate, along a path, now on the 'Ironbridge Way'. Reaching a T-junction turn left, signed 'Ironbridge ¼'. Cross Hodge Bower/Belmont Road and descend to a T-junction; here turn right and continue to descend with a lovely view of the extensive woodland that is such an attractive feature of this area to the left (some of which is explored in Walk 17) and with the roofs of Ironbridge below.

At a T-junction turn right to reach Ironbridge Church (with a view of the Iron Bridge below) and with the church on your left descend steeply. When you reach a row of cream painted houses turn left down a narrow tarmac track, signed Public Footpath, swinging right between houses and descending very steeply. Go left between some very attractive houses to reach the road. Turn left to reach the Iron Bridge and the Tontine Inn (page 130).

✪ *Alternative starting point.*

Leave the town by crossing the Iron Bridge and passing the Toll House Museum and Tourist Information Centre. After a few metres turn left into a car park and walk forward through this, passing the Station Hotel. This is the site of the old Ironbridge station. At the end of the car park join the Severn Valley Way, signed 81 and as a cycleway.

When you reach a gate do not be tempted away to the left but continue through a kissing gate and along the broad track. Approaching another gate look to the left where there is a modern sculpture made of cast iron and made locally and incorporating Celtic symbols. Across the river from here you can see the remains of two old furnaces (the Bedlam Furnaces) built in 1757. These are early examples of blast furnaces designed to use coke instead of coal, a practice made possible by Abraham Darby I's technique developed in Coalbrookdale in 1709 (see Walk 19). Just after passing the Black Swan below on the left go through two gates to reach a road with old railway level crossing gates (Jackfield Sidings) on the left. These were restored in 1999 and originally spanned the Severn Valley line and two sidings that served the many brick and tile works that were in the locality.

Now leaving the old railway line walk along Chapel Road passing Calcutts House (see page 129), then at a junction continue forward, signed 'The Maws Craft Centre', 'Tile Museum' and 'Severn Valley Way'.

The Jackfield Tile Museum occupies the site of the factory in which decorative tiles were made in Victorian times, tiles which adorned palaces, banking halls, and even public lavatories around the world. The tradition of tile making is kept alive here and thousands of examples are displayed.

After about 100 metres pass the Tile Museum on your right (or stop for a visit), then swing left to pass a post-box and along Church Road. Pass Jackfield Church and just past this meet a fence. Pass this and descend a stony track towards the River Severn. *Walking in mid-July I was greeted here by the delightful scent of buddlea.*

Reaching a lane go left along it towards a former pub. Walk to the right of this along a tarmac path to pass on your right (or visit) The Maws Craft Centre, going between wooden posts. Continue along Ferry Road to reach the Boat Inn (page 124) and perhaps some welcome refreshment.

Opposite the pub is a footbridge, taking the place of an earlier ferry. Cross this to reach a disused canal that originally linked the Blists Hill ironworks to the River Severn. We turn right here but you may first wish to visit the Tar Tunnel Museum (with tearooms) that is just ahead.

The Tar Tunnel *is where a remarkable source of natural bitumen was discovered in the eighteenth century. Bitumen was once used to preserve timber and in the manufacture of medicines and fuel oils.*

Ahead you can also see the rails at the end of the Hay Incline Plane down which loaded canal boats were brought before joining the River Severn.

Continuing the walk go along the side of the disused canal, soon crossing it by an iron bridge, and reaching the Coalport China Museum.

The Coalport China Museum *is on the site of the old Coalport China Works. Workshop demonstrations illustrate the activities of the factory and of factory life, and there are superb collections of china on display.*

The Hay Incline Plane

Immediately opposite the museum walk up to the road and turn left along it – passing the 'Beware of Frogs for 300 yards' sign! Just before reaching the Shakespeare Inn turn right along the signed Silkin Way, ascending steps and passing a grove of trees planted to commemorate the Queen's Silver Jubilee in 1977. At the top of the steps, where there is a Silkin Way marker, turn left, signed 'Blists Hill'.

The Silkin Way is a fourteen mile footpath/cycleway, opened in 1977, and named after Lewis Silkin who was responsible after World War II for the Labour Government's rebuilding policy. Part of this was the 1946 New Towns Act which led the creation of some new towns, including Telford, through which the Way passes.

Remains of old furnaces at Blists Hill

When you reach a bridge carrying the Hay Incline Plane do not go under it but turn right up steps, signed 'Sutton Hill' and turn right to walk with the rails of the Hay Incline on your left. At the top of the incline you meet the disused canal and can see the chimney of the powerhouse for the Hay Incline. Continue with the canal on your left to reach a field and warnings of golf balls. However, do not continue through the field but immediately turn left and leave the field along a path, soon with the canal on your left and passing the remains of an old lock. Pass through the corner of the field again and continue with the canal down to your left.

The path swings away from the canal and then, after descending and passing a large industrial car park, brings you to a track along which you turn left to reach the Blists Hill car park with an opportunity for you to visit the Museum and the Victorian Town. *The All Nations Inn is not far away.*

19

A Quaker's Legacy

Ironbridge and Coalbrookdale

Special Feature: The Museum of Iron and Enginuity, Coalbrookdale.

Distance: A: 10 km/6¼ miles; B: 6.2 km/3¾ miles.
Start: Museum of Iron, Coalbrookdale (GR667038).
Alternative Start: Ironbridge High Street (GR671035). Start reading from ✪ on page 139.
Maps: Explorer 242; Landranger 127.
Public Transport: See box on page 130. If starting from Ironbridge start reading from ✪ on page 139.
Car Parking: Museum of Iron, Coalbrookdale (GR67038), or car parks in Ironbridge.
Terrain: Hilly! Some steep descents, stepped but without handrails. Paths good but care needed in walking through The Dingle, especially in a wet period. Good views and lots of fine woodland.
Refreshments: The Grove Inn and the Coalbrookdale Inn, Coalbrookdale; the Tontine Inn and other pubs, teashops and restaurants in Ironbridge.

The Pub
The Coalbrookdale Inn, Coalbrookdale **(CM)**
A superb inn with draught cider and an excellent range of cask ales, regularly changing. Good food (not Mondays) and a very interesting collection of brewing artefacts.

The Museum of Iron is on the site of the historic ironworks where Abraham Darby I, in 1709, first smelted iron with coke instead of charcoal and thereby giving rise to the Industrial Revolution. The museum illustrates the origins of the iron industry and the hard lives of those who worked and lived in the area. It still contains Darby's original blast furnace.

Enginuity, next to the Museum, is Ironbridge's latest attraction. It utilises modern technology to allow visitors to operate and experiment with the exhibits, illustrating thereby how valuable engineering and technology are to our lives today.

Leave the Museum of Iron car park, passing the museum on your right and going through iron gates. Turn left, swing right and after a few metres turn left to ascend steeply, passing a house and then going up steps to the main road. On the left are two pubs, The Grove Inn and The Coalbrookdale Inn.

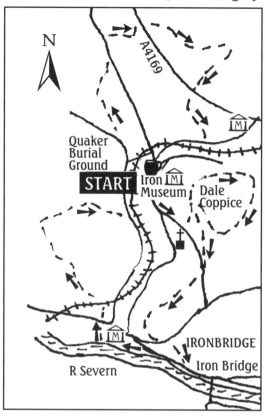

From the steps turn right, then cross the main road to reach Church Road on the left. On the other side of the main road note a fine lamppost that was erected by public subscription to mark the Diamond Jubilee of Queen Victoria in 1897. Turn left along Church Road, passing an 'Except for Access' sign and ascending. Soon reach and go into the churchyard of Coalbrookdale Church through a fine locally made iron gate and walk around the church with a good view across to Benthall Woods (Walk 17) passing the grave of Abraham Darby IV who died in 1878, the fourth member of the illustrious family of ironmakers to carry that name, and the son of the Abraham Darby who was responsible for the Iron Bridge.

Leave the churchyard by steps and through another iron gate, cross the road, go a few metres right and cross a stile on the left to follow a path signed Woodside with 'A Welcome to Dale Coppice'. Walk up through the woods, soon ascending steps.

Reaching a cross-paths, signed Rotunda (*signpost partly obscured by a tree*) you have an opportunity to shorten both the A and B walks by about 1.7 km/1 mile. To do this turn right and now continue reading from ☆ on page 138. Otherwise continue forward up more steps, then, at the top, turn left at a waymark post, soon ascending more steps. Pass a seat decorated with children's drawings on the site of an old cottage, then at a waymark post turn right. At the next waymark turn right and follow the path to enter a grassy area by the side of a gate.

We are now on the former site of opencast workings converted into meadowland, with a fine array of wild flowers and giving some good views of the Ironbridge area. Go forward to join a gravel track and turn left along it for almost 100 metres, then take a waymarked bridleway on the left, initially walking parallel to the gravel track and soon being joined by a path coming in from the right. This seems to be well used by horse-riders and when it swings away to the right continue forward and soon descend towards woodland. Reaching a track turn right, pass a metalled track on the left and soon ascend to meet a fence at a cross-tracks. Here turn right and at a Y-junction of tracks continue forward keeping a fence and woodland over to the left and soon return to the point beside a gate where you entered this area. Go back through the gate and retrace your steps, turning left at the waymark, signed Church Road and left again after a few metres. Pass the seat on the site of the old cottage, then reaching the next waymark post return down steps and on reaching the waymark post signed Rotunda turn left.

The path through Dale Coppice

☆ Soon ascend steps and then eventually descend to meet Church Road again. Cross this and take a path opposite signed Rotunda, going through a squeeze-stile and descending through woodland. At a signposted crosspaths continue forward. Reaching a junction of paths continue forward, signed Rotunda and passing a 'Welcome to Lincoln Hill' sign, to reach a viewpoint on the site of the building named The Rotunda, demolished in 1804. Here turn right down steps and after descending steeply and reaching a waymark post turn right and after a few metres turn left down steps to walk beside a fence. Just past this reach another waymark post and here fork sharp left signed Lincoln Hill Road to walk with a house and a wall on the right. Meeting a driveway continue forward along it to reach a road. Cross this and take a footpath forward to descend, initially down steps, to a road and the river.

If you started from the Iron Bridge turn left to return to your starting point. Otherwise cross the road, turn right and continue reading from ❀ on page 139.

✪ *Alternative starting point:*

Facing the Iron Bridge turn right and walk along the road with the River Severn on your left.

❀ Reaching the Museum of the Gorge (beside which is the Visitor Centre bus stop) descend steps to walk along the river bank, passing the castellated museum built in 1842 as a warehouse by the Coalbrookdale Company, which built the Iron Bridge. Originally there was a wharf here connected by a simple railway to the ironworks in Coalbrookdale (the Ginny Rails), traces of which still remain.

Pass a car park and enter Riverside Park with its beautiful flower displays. After about 50 metres reach a row of trees and turn right to walk with these on your left and flower beds on your right to join a narrow enclosed footpath, passing the Valley Hotel. Reaching a road cross this and walk along Strethill Road, signed as a road used as a public footpath, and walking beside a very attractive house. Go through a gate and carefully cross the railway line. Continue uphill, leaving the tarmac surface to join a tree-lined path that leads into woodland.

Leave the woodland through a gate to have a view of the power station and, more attractively, views to the west of the Long Mynd, Caer Caradoc and other Shropshire hills. Walk with a hedge and fence on the right: leave the field through a gate and immediately turn right through another gate. Continue along an enclosed path to the right of which is Strethill House, once the home of a manager of the Coalbrookdale Factory. The path leads into a driveway along which you continue.

Reaching a house on the left with particularly attractive unspoilt windows, where the driveway swings right, swing slightly left to cross a stile and go down steps into The Dingle. *According to an information board here The Dingle has probably been wooded since the end of the last Ice Age, 15,000 years ago.* Follow the meandering path through woodland ignoring steps on the left, then at a waymark post turn right to descend three steps. The path now swings right and then steeply down more steps. Go right, turn left to pass a grassed area (The Cinder Hill project) where there is a picnic spot and some recently constructed stocks and reach the old Coach Road. Turn left along this and walk with a railway viaduct on your right, passing former factory workers cottages.

Here Walks A and B separate. For the shorter Walk B turn right almost at the end of the viaduct to go under the viaduct and enter the Iron Museum and the main starting point. Note the old locomotives under one of the viaduct arches and don't miss the modern building on the left that contains the remains of Abraham Darby's first furnace. *B walkers who started from Ironbridge now continue reading from the start.*

Continuing Walk A reach a T-junction, turn left along Darby Road and after a few metres reach a footbridge on your right.

*At this point you can make a detour to visit the **Quaker Burial Ground**. Pass the footbridge and continue along Darby Road, passing Rosehill House (another museum), and then at a pottery shop turn left along a waymarked path and climb steps into the Burial Ground. This has now been grassed over and the headstones placed against the walls. Many of the ironmasters and manufacturers were Quakers and were buried here. From the top of the burial ground there is a good view of Coalbrookdale and its wooded hills. Now return down Darby Road to the footbridge to resume the main walk.*

Cross the footbridge over Loamhole Brook and over this turn left along a path through Loamhole Dingle, very shortly descending steps. Walk beside the brook, periodically ascending steps and crossing a footbridge. Reaching descending steps on the left fork right, away from the brook, then after a few metres descend steps, cross another footbridge and ascend steps to follow a steeply ascending path to reach a road. Turn left along this for about 300 metres and, reaching an outcrop of rock, turn right along a stony track signed Crackshall Lane.

Approaching a house on the right enter woodland, soon ascending a steep flight of wooden steps. At a T-junction of paths turn left, again waymarked Crackshall Lane, and reaching a stile cross this and turn left along Crackshall Lane to meet the main road. Cross this carefully and walk forward along an initially tarmacked track, passing Severn Cottage on the left. Passing a pylon and under a double row of power cables the track swings left and after about 200 metres passes under the cables again. Just under the second line of these turn right over a stile and down into a field, taking care at the bottom of the slope for a little ankle-twisting ditch that may not be apparent if the grass is high. Walk with a hedge on the left, then, when the hedge ends swing right, aiming towards the left-hand corner of a wood. Meeting the wood walk with it on your right to reach a road via a stile.

Cross the road, cross Crackshall Lane (confusing, isn't it!) and join a driveway, signed The Old Wynd House. Just before this, on the right, at the corner with Crackshall Lane, you will see the remains of a stile. Before the road was built a footpath emerged here and if you look over the stile, towards the left, you should be able to see a now filled-in canal bridge. The canal, met on Walk 18, ran here and as you walk along the driveway the remains of it are on the other side of the hedge on your right. It terminated at The Old Wynd House from where an inclined plane (similar to the one met on Walk 18) took trucks to and from a lower level.

Swing left beside the house, cross a stile between sheds and continue forward along a path, signed Cherry Tree Hill, to soon reach a Severn Gorge Countryside Trust welcome to The Old Wynd.

Here you have a choice of routes.

If you turn right along a permissive footpath and descend steps you will come to a steeply descending stepped path following the line of the inclined plane. You might like to go down this path and then, at the bottom, cross Cherry Tree Hill and turn left along it for about 200 metres to meet the alterative route coming in on the left.

Otherwise stay on, or return to, the original path and descend to reach and cross Cherry Tree Hill and turn left along it. *About 150 metres further along the road is the Museum of Steel Structures.*

The Iron Museum

After a few metres turn right to descend steps and follow an enclosed path, crossing the railway. Pass a large pool, another reservoir that provided water power to the ironworks. Cross a sluice and after a few metres turn sharp right to enter Woodside Orchard (a local community project). Follow the gravel path to leave the orchard through a gate and turn right along a path. Join a road coming in from the left and reach a main road. Cross this to join Darby Road and return to the railway viaduct. Go under the viaduct again, turn left and after a few metres turn left once more under the viaduct to reach the Iron Museum, topped with a fine clock dated 1843, and the 'Enginuity' exhibition and the main starting point. Note the old locomotives under one of the viaduct arches and don't miss the modern building on the left that contains the remains of Abraham Darby's first furnace.

If you started from the Iron Bridge now continue reading from page 136.

20

Two Great Rivers

Tewkesbury

Special Features: The confluence of the Rivers Avon and Severn; Tewkesbury town tour; Tewkesbury museums.

Distance: A: 14.4km/9 miles; B: 12km/7½ miles.
Start: Tewkesbury High Street (GR893331).
Maps: Explorer 190; Landranger 150.
Car Parking: Oldbury Road car park, Tewkesbury (Oldbury Road runs parallel to the High Street) (GR894331).
Public Transport: 1) Rail to Ashchurch, then bus service 41 to Tewkesbury. Leave the bus in the High Street at Boots.
2) Rail to Cheltenham, bus service D/E to town centre, then service 41 to Tewkesbury. Leave the bus in the High Street at the Anchor Inn. There are also bus services from Gloucester, Worcester and Evesham.
Terrain: One minor hill but otherwise flat and easy walking along field paths, quiet lanes and riversides.
Refreshments: Pubs in Twyning and Tewkesbury. Plenty of other refreshment opportunities in Tewkesbury.

The Pubs

The Fleet Inn, Twyning
A fourteenth or fifteenth century riverside pub and a delightful place to stop on a fine sunny day. Popular with diners. Good cask ales.
Ye Olde Black Bear, Tewkesbury
The Black Bear dates back to 1308 and claims to be the oldest inn in Tewkesbury. Most of the present structure is early sixteenth century. Food and good cask ales.
The Berkeley Arms, Tewkesbury **(GBG) (CM)**
A fine sixteenth century Grade II listed building with food and good cask ales

Tewkesbury has a long and impressive history. Artefacts, now in Tewkesbury Museum, provide evidence that the area was occupied in Roman and Saxon times. Tewkesbury Abbey (see walk 21) was founded in the eleventh century, probably replacing an earlier church. Tewkesbury became a Free Borough by a charter of the Earls of Gloucester, this status being confirmed by a charter of Elizabeth I in 1574. After the Civil War a new charter (now in the Museum) was granted by William III.

In 1471 the Lancastrian cause in the Wars of the Roses (see also walks 21 and 9) was lost when Edward, Prince of Wales, son of Henry VI was killed in a battle south of the town.

The two rivers, the Avon and the Severn, have had a great influence on the development of the town and traffic along these led to its increasing prosperity as a market town. The Severn had been used since Roman times, and the Avon became navigable in the seventeenth century. Flour milling, using waterpower, was well established by the early eighteenth century when about thirty stagecoaches a day passed through the town. However, Tewkesbury missed many of the benefits of the Industrial Revolution for it was by-passed by the railways. Much of the town's industry (nail making, tanning and stocking making) left and it remained seemingly frozen in time from the middle of the eighteenth century until World War II. This, however, is responsible for many features that make it such a fascinating town to explore today.

Although leading to much of its early development the rivers also acted as a constraint. Tewkesbury is situated above the flood plain and frequent flooding of the surrounding areas acted as a barrier to its physical expansion. This had two significant effects that we can see today. Additional stories were added to a number of buildings making them much taller than might be expected. And towards the end of the seventeenth century the areas behind houses fronting the streets became building plots, accessed by alleyways and steadily filled by small dwellings. These became increasingly squalid with cholera and diphtheria being rife in the nineteenth century. Many of these alleys remain, some having linked together to form courts. The squalid buildings have gone and they now contain some attractive houses.

Starting from the High Street walk along Clark's Alley which is about 20 metres to the left of the Tudor House Hotel (when facing the Hotel).

Tudor House Hotel. This dates from 1540 and contains a priest's hiding hole. It once housed the 'Dissenter's Academy' for learned men who were unable to go to university because they were not members of the Church of England. The mock-Tudor frontage was added in Victorian times. It became a hotel after the First World War.

In Clark's Alley note the raised brickwork, similar to that seen along canal towpaths and designed to prevent horses from slipping – and presumably here for the same reason.

Turn left beside the Mill Avon, then right over a bridge erected in 1822 and leading to Healings Mill.

The Mill Avon links the Avon (at Upper Lode) with the Severn (at Lower Lode). Its origins are unknown but it is thought to have been

143

dug in Saxon times, possibly to provide waterpower for mills. The Domesday Book records two mills along it, and in the late sixteenth century there were four. Healings Mill is the only remaining working mill: there has been a mill on this site since the thirteenth century, the present building dating from 1865. Abbey Mill, that we shall meet later, is now a restaurant.

Turn right past the mill – the River Avon can be seen over to the left – now joining the Severn Way. Pass a lock linking the Avon and the Mill Avon and on reaching King John's Bridge ascend steps to reach the road.

King John's Bridge. *King John ordered a bridge to be built here at the end of the twelfth century, and provided for its upkeep. It was a narrow stone bridge with a long*

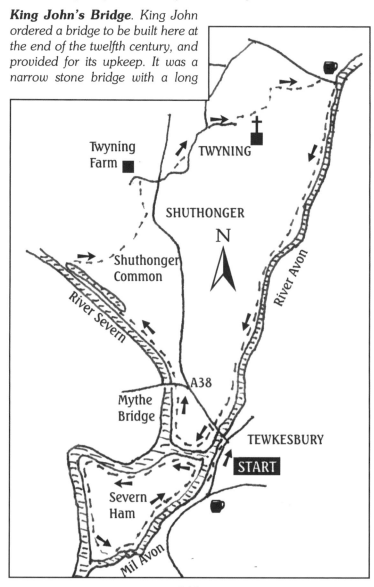

wooden causeway, but the causeway has been replaced by an earth embankment and the bridge considerably widened.

Turn left and cross Beaufort Bridge over the Avon, turn left to cross a stile and then left again to walk beside the river. Pass a fenced reservoir and reach the junction of the Avon and the Severn, then pass the Severn-Trent Waterworks. Reaching the elegant Mythe Bridge, designed by Thomas Telford in 1826, leave the Severn Way (which continues over the bridge) and go under the bridge. Pass a fine stone-built house, originally a tollhouse, and continue beside the river for just over half a mile/nearly a kilometre to reach Mythe Pool and now walk between this and the river. At the end of the pool cross a stile, turn right, then right again over another stile to walk diagonally left, crossing yet another stile. Continue your bearing diagonally right across the field (east), go through a gate and over a footbridge and walk straight forward, passing a caravan park on the left. Ascend steps, cross a stile and walk with a fence on the left through Shuthonger Common with a good view of Bredon Hill ahead.

Reaching a house cross a stile and go forward along a driveway, then about 50 metres before reaching the A38 turn left along an enclosed footpath beside Bell Cottage. Leave the path by a gate and turn right to walk with a hedge on the right. Go through a kissing-gate and walk with a fence on the right, very shortly going through another kissing-gate and walking with the fence on the left. To the left you will have, if the weather is good, an excellent view of the complete range of the Malvern Hills. Go through a gate and turn right along a lane, cross the A38 and continue along the lane, signed Church End. After almost a 100 metres leave the road through a kissing-gate on the left (*or you can continue along the lane as we shall rejoin it soon*) and walk with houses and a fence on the right. Go through two more kissing-gates and then diagonally left, passing a power pole. Go through another two kissing-gates to rejoin the lane and turn left along it, then turn right at a T-junction, signed Church End, to reach the Church of St Mary Magdalene.

The Church of St Mary Magdalene, Twyning. *There has been a church at Twyning since Saxon times. The original site is not known but is thought to be under or near the present church, which was built about 1100. Numerous changes have since been made but a number of older features remain, notably the eleventh century buttresses in the nave and the Norman doorway. Niches on either side would, until the Reformation, have contained religious effigies: on the left are the remains of a stoup for holy water. The tower and windows are thirteenth century. There are two impressive monuments, one on the south wall of the chancel to Sybil Clare who died in 1575, a second on the south wall of the tower vestry to the Hancock family who were seventeenth century merchants. On the wall of the nave adjacent to the chancel is a blocked doorway, possibly Saxon, that could have been a priest's door to an earlier*

Twyning Church

chancel or sanctuary. Much more information can be found in a booklet on sale in the church.

Continue along the road and at the end cross a stile and walk along an enclosed path to cross another stile into a field. Swing right, passing a pool on the left, then veer left to go under power lines with another pool to your right. Ahead you will see a broken row of poplars, with some newly planted conifers that will eventually fill in the gaps (or perhaps replace the poplars). Aim to the left of the rightmost fifteen of the older trees (about the middle of the field boundary ahead) and here cross a stile and turn left along a broad track.

At the end of the row of poplars turn right over a stile and walk down the left-hand edge of the field, now having a good view of the Cotswolds. Pass a footbridge on the left, go through a kissing-gate and turn left to walk with a fence on the right, cross a stile and go diagonally right to cross another stile and continue your bearing to go through a gate. Turn left and walk

The Fleet Inn

146

with a fence and houses on the left: in the corner of the field cross a stile on the left and follow an enclosed path to reach a road and turn right along this to reach the Fleet Inn.

The Fleet Inn is built on a site that was home to ferrymen for a thousand years, probably longer. The ferry was in use until recently but on my last visit it had, sadly, closed. It may perhaps be re-opened. The old building dates from the fourteenth or fifteenth centuries with the inglenook fireplace in the bar dating from around 1500. The ferryman's cottage became an alehouse and when licensing of premises was introduced in 1751 this alehouse became known as The Fleet. The buildings have been extended and extensively modernised and the exterior is now largely early nineteenth century, formed from three cottages built probably in the seventeenth or eighteenth century.

From the inn, turn right across grass to cross a footbridge and go through a kissing gate, then walk with a fence on the left to go through another kissing gate. After about 50 metres you pass on the right the ancient Chad Well, surrounded by a fence.

The Chad Well (actually a spring capped by a stone basin) had an ancient reputation for the treatment of eye complaints. It is thought that it was linked with St Chad who had a monastic cell in Pershore in the seventh century.

You now have about 3 km/1¾ miles to go along the river back to Tewkesbury. The river is well used by pleasure craft , swans and water lilies adding to its appeal. Ahead you will soon see the tower of Tewkesbury Abbey. Nearing Tewkesbury and approaching a fence and a row of trees, including two oaks, the path moves away from the river to a stile about 50 metres to the right of the left-hand corner of the field. Cross this and a stone footbridge and go forward to pass under a bridge of the old railway, closed in 1961, that originally linked Ashchurch, Tewkesbury and Upton-upon-Severn. Go forward to reach the road and turn left to go over Beaufort Bridge and reach King John's Bridge. Ahead is Ye Olde Black Bear and you can, if you want to end your walk there, turn right along the High Street back to the starting point.

The Black Bear dates back to 1308 and claims to be the oldest inn in Tewkesbury. Most of the present structure is early sixteenth century. It is a wonderful rambling building with immense historical interest.

Otherwise go down the steps by the bridge and walk back along the Mill Avon, then left over the bridge. Turn right for about 75 metres and cross the Mill Avon again by a footbridge onto the Severn Ham.

The Severn Ham is an island of meadowland between the Severn and the Mill Avon and is a Site of Special Scientific Interest. It contains some rare plant species and is an important breeding area for redshank, corn bunting and water associated birds. An Act of Parliament of 1808 regulates Commoners Rights to sell the pasturage after the hay is cut by 12 July. The rights are vested in Trustees, town councillors and elected representatives of dwellings fronting the three main streets of the town. These occupiers are entitled to a share of the sale (by auction) of the pasturage after costs of maintaining the Ham have been met.

Here the A and B walks separate. (*Some of the paths on the Ham are permissive paths.*) For the shorter B walk turn left and walk beside the Mill Avon for about 400 metres to reach a footbridge and a sluice. Pass this for a few metres to observe an old waterwheel on Abbey Mill, then return to the footbridge and continue reading from ✷ below.

Continuing the A walk go forward along a gravel track and follow it to reach the Avon. Turn left to walk beside it, parallel to our outward walk on the opposite side. Soon pass a fenced reservoir on the left and meet the confluence with the River Severn once more. Approaching a lock and passing a river lock sign continue forward through trees and follow the permissive path round beside the river and soon pass a weir.

Eventually reach an apparent Y-junction and take the left fork (the forward section, at the time of writing, being a blind alley) to move away from the river, but very soon meet the Mill Avon and walk beside it with Tewkesbury Abbey directly ahead. Soon pass a seat and, after passing a pipe bridge, walk parallel to the incoming route of walk 21 on the opposite side of the river. Approaching a sluice and a footbridge note an old waterwheel on Abbey Mill.

✷ Immediately cross the Mill Avon by the footbridge to pass Abbey Mill, noting the attractive timber-framed cottages ahead.

Abbey Mill. *The first mill was built around 1190 for the Priory of Tewkesbury and was operated by Benedictine monks on corn supplied by local farmers. It was rebuilt in 1793. Healing's Mill, that we passed at the start of the walk, was built in 1865 and it is thought that this led to the decline of Abbey Mill which ceased operations in 1920. It is a Grade II listed building and is now occupied by a restaurant.*

Abbey Mill is sometimes known as Fletcher's Mill, named after a character in 'John Halifax, Gentleman' by Dinah Craik (1826-1887), a once very popular book but which now seems not to appeal to modern tastes. In the book, the narrator is sitting with the young John Halifax, where
"... one could see a goodly sweep of country. First, close below, flowed the Avon – Shakspeare's Avon – here a narrow, sluggish stream, but capable ... of being roused into fierceness and foam. Now it slipped on quietly enough, contenting itself with turning a flour-mill hard by, the lazy whirr of which made a sleepy, incessant monotone which I was fond of hearing.

From the opposite bank stretched a wide green level, called the Ham – dotted with pasturing cattle of all sorts. Beyond it was a second river, forming an arch of a circle round the verdant flat. But the stream itself lay so low as to be invisible from where we sat; you could only trace the line of its course by the small white sails that glided in and out, oddly enough, from behind clumps of trees, and across meadow lands.

They attracted John's attention. 'Those can't be boats, surely. Is there water there?'

'To be sure, or you would not see the sails. It is the Severn; though at this distance you can't perceive it; yet it is deep enough too, as you may see by the boats it carries. You would hardly believe so, to look at it here – but I believe it gets broader and broader, and turns out a noble river by the time it reaches the King's Roads, and forms the Bristol Channel.'"

Immediately past the Abbey Mill turn right briefly for a few metres to see the remains of another waterwheel. Walk forward up Mill Street, to reach the Bell Hotel and Church Street.

The Bell Hotel *was once a monastery guest house and dates back to the thirteenth century. Over the doorway note the inscription I K 1696.*

Opposite is the entrance to Tewkesbury Abbey, visited in walk 21 (see page 156). Turn left and after about 50 metres pass Chandler's Court, with sixteenth and fifteenth century buildings either side. Opposite is the medieval timber-framed British Legion Club. Now turn left down Old Baptist Chapel Court to pass the chapel (open to the public) and reach the old burial ground.

The Baptist movement *was well established in Tewkesbury in the seventeenth century although members were subject to persecution by the State, many being imprisoned and some sentenced to death. This persecution perhaps explains the location of the chapel in a concealed alleyway. Proceedings would have had to be carried out in secrecy but the location being so close to the Abbey would suggest intense religious conviction.*

It is not certain when the chapel was first used for worship but records exist dating back to 1655. The building is fifteenth century when it was a house with much the same structure as exists now. A new larger chapel was opened in the town in 1805, a more tolerant time. The old chapel was acquired by Tewkesbury Borough Council in 1976 and restored to show how it would have appeared in about 1720.

Now return to Church Street and turn left. On the opposite side of Church Street is the Merchant's House (The Little Museum), a restored house showing a merchant's house as it would have been in the early Tudor period. Next to it is the John Moore Countryside Museum.

The John Moore Countryside Museum is housed in a fifteenth century timber-framed building, part of a row of restored cottages (Nos. 34-39 and 41-49). It has three floors of natural history and is open (modest admission fee) April-October, Tues-Sats 10am-1pm, 2pm-5pm; and Bank Holidays and most Saturdays in winter.

Pass Smith's Court on the left and another entrance to the Abbey on the right. On the left pass another fine building, probably fourteenth century, now occupied by Pickwick's of Tewkesbury. Immediately past this turn left down Turner's Court. Reaching tarmac turn right passing several timber-framed buildings to reach Church Street again opposite the Abbey School. On your right is a fourteenth century building and on its right one built in the sixteenth century. Turn left along Church Street to pass the Royal Hop Pole Hotel and Post Office Lane on the left.

The Royal Hop Pole Hotel: This fifteenth century half-timbered inn is thought to be one of the oldest inns in Gloucestershire. It backs onto the Mill Avon where it has some attractive gardens and its own private moorings. Charles Dickens came here and mentions it in 'The Pickwick Papers' – there is a quotation on the wall outside the hotel.

Just before reaching a pedestrian crossing pass the striking house No.100.

This building carries the inscription B R K 1664 (the year when it was probably re-built). It is known as the Hat Shop because of the large beadle's hat hanging outside. Records show that it housed a glover's shop in 1685.

Cross the road by the pedestrian crossing to the Berkeley Arms.

The Berkeley Arms is a superb sixteenth century Grade II listed building with the oldest facade in the town. On the front range of windows (and on the building next door) some fifteenth century tracery can be seen. At the rear is a medieval timber-framed barn, believed to be the oldest non-ecclesiastical building in the town, and used by the pub as a dining area.

On the right of the Berkeley Arms an alleyway (open only when the inn is open) leads to the impressive timbered entrance to the lounge. On the right of the adjacent building is Lilley's Alley. Go down here to view the fifteenth century Tudor Cottage and, just beyond it the house named 'Claypipes', so named because the alley once contained the drying racks for clay pipes that were made here. Close to the Berkeley Arms is Warwick House, timber-framed with a triple overhang.

Continue back past (or to visit) the Berkeley Arms, pass the war memorial and the present Methodist Church and follow the road round along Barton Street, passing several alleys, including: Chapel Court *(this lead to the Baptist Chapel built in 1805. There was originally the entrance to an inn here and if you go a little way down you will see on the right part of its balustrade)*; Compton's Alley *(the Compton family had a furniture shop and two ledgers of the business found in the roof are now in the Tewkesbury Museum*); Hughes Alley (*he was a milkman who kept his cows on Perry Hill where John Wesley preached on several occasions*); Fish Alley (*possibly so named because most of the inhabitants were fishermen*), Yarnell's Alley (*a chair maker who supported the French Revolution and was known as Jacobite Yarnell*) to reach the Tewkesbury Museum.

Tewkesbury Museum *is housed in a very old building, parts of which are thought to date back to the fifteenth century. After the Civil War it seems to have had a wealthy occupant who converted it from what had originally been two cottages. It contains an extensive collection of material relating to the history of the town: the Battle Room contains a diorama depicting the Battle of Tewkesbury in 1471 (the 'Bloody Meadow' is visited in walk 21).*

Return back along Barton Street, cross Church Road by the pedestrian crossing and turn left, passing No. 100 again, then right along Post Office Lane. Turn right, then after about 40 metres right again along Prior's Alley (*probably having a connection with the Abbey*) to join Tolzey Lane and turn right passing more timber-framed buildings to meet the High Street. On the right is the sixteenth century Cross House.

Cross House *is thought to be the site of the Court House of the Lords of Tewkesbury. It has a fine entrance and contains a Tudor staircase and some Elizabethan panelled rooms.*

Opposite is a remarkable old building, now a barber's shop. Turn left and pass the 'House of the Nodding Gables', now occupied by the Halifax Building Society.

This is also known as the House of the Golden Key and has a large key hanging outside. It is a Tudor building, and when a fourth storey was added the stress broke some of the attic ridges and caused the two gables of the roof to topple forward to form the 'Nodding Gables'.

On the opposite side of the road is Clarence House, built in the early sixteenth century. A fourth floor was added in the late seventeenth century and the half-timbered façade was covered by extensive plasterwork. Continuing along High Street shortly pass an 1838 building carrying a good coat of arms; opposite are two more buildings of note: Berkeley Antiques and the Nottingham Arms. Pass Machine Court and Nortonbury House, occupied by the Gloucestershire Echo, then the Anchor Inn (1774) to reach the bus stop or continue past Care's Alley to the Tudor House Hotel and cross the road to return to the car park.

21

Tewkesbury's Bloody Meadow

Tewkesbury

Special Features: The Wars of the Roses Battlefield; Odda's Chapel, Deerhurst; Tewkesbury Abbey; The Priory Church of St Mary at Deerhurst.

Distance: A: 12 km/7½ miles; B: 7.75 km/4¾ miles.
Start: Tewkesbury Abbey (GR891324).
Maps: Explorer 190, 179; Landranger 150.
Car Parking: Pay and display car park near to the Abbey at the junction of Church Street and Gander Lane. If full there is another park a little further down Gander Lane.
Public Transport: 1) Rail to Ashcurch, then bus service 41 to Tewkesbury. Leave the bus at Tewkesbury Abbey.
2) Rail to Cheltenham, bus service D/E to town centre, then service 41 to Tewkesbury. Leave the bus at Tewkesbury Abbey.
There are also bus services from Gloucester, Worcester and Evesham.
Terrain: Some undulations but mostly easy walking on field paths and along the River Severn.
Refreshments: The Coalhouse Inn, Apperley; several pubs, teashops and restaurants in Tewkesbury.

The Pubs

Coalhouse Inn, Apperley (Walk A only)
A welcoming riverside inn with food and some good cask ales. Closed Mondays except bank holidays.
The Berkeley Arms, Church Street, Tewkesbury. **(GBG) (CM)**
A fine half-timbered sixteenth century Grade II listed building. A barn at the rear is believed to be the oldest non-ecclesiastical building in the town. Food and good cask ales.

From Church Street walk to the left of the entrance to the Abbey along Gander Lane. Cross the River Swilgate and passing a car park on the left turn right to enter parkland through a kissing gate and walk beside the river with a good view of the Abbey on your right. Reaching a main road, cross this carefully and walk along Lower Lode Lane. Pass some steps on the left and after about another 250 metres turn left along a path, cross a stile on the right and walk through the 'Bloody Meadow' keeping a hedge on your left.

The Bloody Meadow is believed to be the scene, during the Battle of Tewkesbury (1471) in the Wars of the Roses, of a massacre of the panicking Lancastrian forces as they tried to escape across the River Swilgate that is over to your right. The result of the battle was to put the House of York kings on the throne until 1485 when Richard III was killed at the Battle of Bosworth (See Walk 9). In the meadow, willow, whitethorn, redthorn and alder trees have been planted to commemorate those who died in the battle. A brick mounted information panel at the exit from the meadow gives more information about the battle.

Leave the meadow onto a road along which you turn right to reach the entrance to Tewkesbury Park Hotel, Golf and Country Club. Follow the driveway until it starts to veer right towards the golf house and here fork diagonally left across grass towards and through a hedge gap which leads into another golf area. Here turn right and walk along the right-hand edge of the golf area with the remains of a hedge on your right, soon passing a wooden practice range suitable for bad weather.

At the end of the hedge continue straight forward to cross a footbridge and a stile and continue through a field with a hedge on your left, almost immediately ignoring a way-marked path on your left. Cross a stile and continue forward through a second field: at the end of this do not go through the gate but turn right to

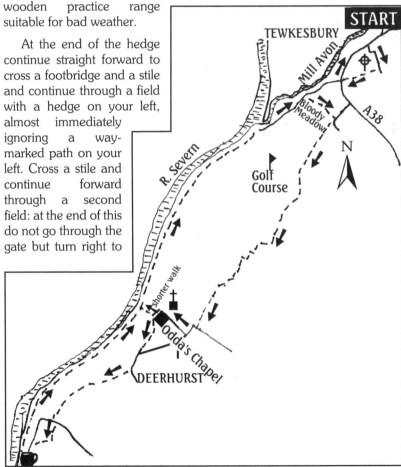

walk with woodland on your left, the path soon swinging left to follow the edge of the woodland. Leave the field by a stile and then immediately go right, go through a gate and turn left to walk with a fence on the left. Follow this as it swings right to reach another stile; cross this (it was redundant when I was last here) and walk with a fence on the left.

Passing Park Farm, walk with a garden and a ha-ha (a low wall and ditch) on your left, then with a hedge, to reach, after about 75 metres, a stile on the left of a gateway. Cross this, turn right and now walk with a hedge on your right, following it as it bends left, then right. Cross a stile and descend to walk with a hedge on the right, following this as it bends left, then right. Just before it starts to bend left again cross a stile on the right. Go straight forward across a field to cross a footbridge and turn left, now walking with a hedge on your left. Then cross three stiles to reach a road and turn right along this.

Follow the road as it bends left passing Deerhurst Priory, then at a T-junction turn right signed Odda's Chapel. You soon reach the Priory Church of St. Mary, Deerhurst, a visit to which is strongly recommended.

The Priory Church of St. Mary is a Saxon foundation dating from AD700. It is rich in history with what is probably the finest Saxon font in existence. This was discovered over a hundred years ago in a local farm where it was being used as a drinking trough!

Saxon font in St Mary's Church

There is an interesting Victorian window to the Strickland family in the north-west end of the church. Below this are the arms of the family with a turkey-cock crest; a member of the family sailed to America with John Cabot and on his return imported the first turkeys into England.

At the east end of the north aisle a brass on the floor is to the memory of Sir John Casey and his wife. He died in 1400 and was 'Chief Baron of the Exchequer to Our Lord the King'. Victorian plaster has been stripped from the wall to expose the Saxon masonry.

There is much more of interest to see and the guide book and information sheets available inside are strongly recommended.

Plaque in Odda's Chapel

Leave by the front entrance passing the attractive fourteenth century farm attached to the church, which was probably once a dormitory for the monks of the priory.

Now continue your former route passing a metal flood barrier: ahead you will see a flood level indicator. The tarmac now swings left and passes Odda's Barn to reach Odda's Chapel.

Odda's Chapel is a Saxon chapel that was built in 1056 by Odda, a kinsman of Edward the Confessor, and now in the care of English Heritage. This is an almost complete example of a Saxon building. In the sixteenth century a timber-framed farmhouse was attached to it and the chapel was used as the farmhouse kitchen. Its origins were eventually forgotten and only rediscovered during repairs to the house in 1885.

Now continue past the chapel for a few metres when Walk A and Walk B separate.

For the shorter Walk B turn right through a gate and follow a broad track to reach the River Severn near to a massive oak. Turn right and now continue reading from ✪ *on page 156.*

Continuing Walk A turn left to cross a stile. Walk forward across the field and cross a stile to the left of three large willows. Then go forward aiming about 50 metres to the right of the house that you can see ahead and cross a stile beside a gate. Turn right along the road passing 'Byways' and 'Lower Meadow' and when the road swings left cross a stile ahead. Here there are two waymarked paths: one going left, one going straight ahead. Take the one ahead and cross the field to a stile about 30 metres to the left of two large oaks.

Over the stile go diagonally left up the hill and, over the hill, continue forward aiming for the far right-hand corner of the field where you enter woodland. Descend through this, cross a stile and turn left to walk along a narrow field with a hedge and stream over to the right. Leave the field in its far left corner through two gates. Pass a footpath on the right, and go straight ahead along the driveway of a large white house, passing a duck pond on the right and reaching a road. Turn left along this for a few metres and then ascend steps and cross a stile on the right. Follow the right-hand boundary of the field until you reach a stile on the right. Cross this and go diagonally left to join a lane via a stile. Turn left and follow the lane for about 200 metres to reach the Coalhouse Inn. The inn has a pleasant garden overlooking the river.

> **Coalhouse Inn**. *There was originally a wharf here to which coal was brought via the Severn from the South Wales collieries. This ceased when the Coombe Hill Canal, now derelict, was built in 1796 specifically to carry coal to Cheltenham.*

After leaving the inn cross the grass in front of the inn onto tarmac, turn right along this and cross a stile.

> *You are now following the **Severn Way**, the waymark symbol of which is a Severn Trow. These were large barges with a shallow draft (the river is very shallow in places) but gangs of men were still required to pull them over some of the rock shallows. The Severn Way, the longest riverside walk in Britain, follows the course of the river from its source on Plynlimon in North Wales to Severn Beach, close to where the river joins the Bristol Channel.*

Across the river you should have a good view of the Malverns. At the first stile note the sign 'No Elvering' (elvers are young eels), pass a pool on the right and now follow the Severn Way towards Tewkesbury.

✪ *Walk B joins Walk A on the riverside path.*

Ahead Bredon Hill with its tower comes into view (if the weather is clear). Approaching Tewkesbury, the woodland that you have been passing on the right starts to pull in and you reach a boathouse. The Severn now swings away left and is joined by the Mill Avon (see page 143). Cross a driveway and go through a parking area, then follow a short section of footpath into a picnic area. However you cannot follow the Mill Avon as there is no footpath so swing right to leave the area through a gate onto the road. Turn left along this and on reaching the A38 cross this carefully.

If you wish at this point to return directly to your car go through the kissing gate and retrace your steps back to the car park. Otherwise turn left and shortly, on reaching Abbey Precinct, turn right along a driveway. Just before reaching an impressive archway turn left to enter the grounds of the Abbey.

> **Tewkesbury Abbey** *(the Abbey Church of St Mary the Virgin) was founded at the end of the eleventh century as a Benedictine Monastery. The spectacular central tower, dating from the early part of the twelfth century, is 148 feet high and is the largest surviving Norman central tower in existence. From the top are panoramic views of the Avon and Severn valleys, the Malvern Hills and, on a fine day, the Welsh mountains.*

Tewkesbury Abbey

Above the outer arch of the Norman North Porch is a modern sculpture of the Vigin Mary; the massive doors are almost certainly the original ones from 1121. Tewkesbury Abbey is the second largest parish church in England but has the grandeur of a cathedral. The interior displays two distinct architectural styles; twelfth century Norman with heavy walls, thick columns and round arches; fourteenth century Decorated with pointed arches and ribs of stone in intricate patterns.

With the exception of Westminster Abbey, Tewkesbury contains more medieval tombs than any other church in Britain and monuments to the historic families of the De Glares and Despencers abound. The south transept has a Raphael painting which once hung at Versailles. The abbey possesses three organs. One is known as the Milton Organ; it was built for Magdalen College, Oxford and derives its name from the belief that Milton played upon it while he was secretary to Cromwell.

Leaving the Abbey walk along the main entranceway with six yew trees on each side. Leave through the beautifully decorated entrance gate and turn right passing the Abbey Refectory, fronted by a modern sculpture. Pass, or visit, the John Moore Countryside Museum (see page 150) to reach the bus stop or to turn right along Gander Lane for the car park. Continue forward along Church Street for the Berkeley Arms.

Index

More walks from Meridian...

A YEAR OF WALKS IN THE THREE CHOIRS COUNTIES by Roy Woodcock

The Three Choirs Counties comprise Herefordshire, Gloucestershire and Worcertertshire and this selection of walks takes twelve widely distributed locations, one for each month of the year.

£6.95. ISBN 1-869922-51-4. 112 pages. 28 illustrations. 12 maps

WALKS IN SEVERN COUNTRY by Roy Woodcock

The River Severn, Britain's longest river, rises on the slopes of Plynlimon in Wales and flows through the beautiful counties of Powys, Shropshire, Worcestershire and Gloucestershire before discharging into the Bristol Channel. In this book the author presents twenty walks that explore some of the fine towns and countryside that the Severn passes through on its 220 mile journey to the sea.

£7.95. ISBN 1-869922-49-2. 128 pages. 37 illustrations. 20 maps

WALKS TO WET YOUR WHISTLE by Roger Seedhouse

Eighteen walks covering some of the most beautiful countryside in Shropshire and along its Staffordshire borders, each providing an opportunity to visit a pub in which the walker will feel welcome and comfortable.

£6.95. ISBN 1 869922 41 7. 112 pages. 17 photographs. 18 maps.

MORE WALKS TO WET YOUR WHISTLE by Roger Seedhouse

A second collection of walks with a pub in Shropshire and along its Staffordshire borders.

£6.95. ISBN 1 869922 36 0. 112 pages. 24 photographs. 18 maps.

WARWICKSHIRE WALKS TO WET YOUR WHISTLE by Roger Seedhouse

Roger Seedhouse's third collection of walks, all with good pubs, in Warwickshire – a land of lakes and country parks which are a delight to behold, merging into the Northern Cotswolds with its buildings of honey-hued stone.

£8.95. ISBN 1-869922-48-4 120 pages 21 photos 20 maps

WALKS THROUGH HISTORY IN THE HEART OF ENGLAND by Roger Seedhouse

The Heart of England is rich in history, both ancient and more modern, and the twenty-four walks in this book will offer the enquiring walker many intriguing glimpses of a bygone age – with iron-age forts, battle sites, medieval castles and even a second world war camp. All of them start at, or pass through, places of historical interest that will add greatly to your appreciation of a day out in beautiful walking country.

£8.95 ISBN 1-869922-41-7. 160 pages. 38 photos. 24 maps.

All Meridian titles are available from booksellers or, if in difficulty, direct from the publishers.

Please send your remittance, including the following amounts for postage and packing:
Order value up to £10.00 add £1.50;
over £10.00 and up to £20.00 add £2.50;
over £20.00 add £3.00.

Meridian Books
Sales Office
8 Hartside Close, Lutley, Halesowen, West Midlands B63 1HP
Tel: 0121-429 4397
e-mail: meridian.books@tiscali.co.uk

Please send for our complete catalogue of walking guides covering both local and long distance walks.